The Year 'Round Quotebook

Special Occasion Resources for Newsletters, Bulletins, Talks, and Sermons

E. C. McKenzie

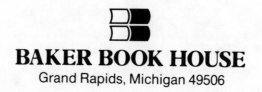

BAKER BOOK HOUSE

Grand Rapids, Michigan 49506

ISBN: 0-8010-6184-9

Second printing, July 1987

These quotations were selected from
Mac's Giant Book of Quips and Quotes.

Printed in the United States of America

Contents

January

New Year's Day

Many Americans no longer celebrate the arrival of the New Year — they celebrate the survival of the old year.

There's only one good thing that can be said for bad habits. If it weren't for them we couldn't make New Year's resolutions.

Many people look forward to the new year for a new start on old habits.

The New Year gives people a fresh start on their old habits.

The New Year is when some people drop in for a call and others call in for a drop.

The New Year is like a new baby — many changes will be necessary, some of which may be neglected.

What the New Year brings us will depend a great deal on what we bring to the New Year.

New Year's Eve is when you take your wife out, and she takes you back home.

A New Year's resolution is a promise to stop doing everything you enjoy most.

Serious trouble comes when the New Year's resolutions collide with the old year's habits.

Why not be sure by having your New Year's resolutions notorized?

Most of the leaves we turned over in January have already started to fall.

A New Year's resolution is something that goes in one year and out the other.

May your troubles in the coming New Year be as short-lived as your resolutions.

A New Year's resolution is a promise to stop doing everything you enjoy most.

Every year many American girls resolve that they're going to give up rich foods and poor boyfriends.

If you kept every resolution you made last year, you'd probably be skinny, smart, healthy, rich — and bored.

A resolution is always stronger at its birth than at any subsequent period.

We should keep all our resolutions secret. That way nobody will know when we break them.

The fragments of broken resolutions can be cemented together, but the cracks will show.

5

February

Lincoln's Birthday

I recognize the sublime truth announced in the Holy Scriptures and proven by all history that those nations only are blessed whose God is the Lord.   —Abraham Lincoln

An elderly gentleman in Nevada calls his car Abe. It's a Lincoln.

Abraham Lincoln had great difficulty getting an education — but what can you expect from a guy who didn't play football or basketball?

Abraham Lincoln was great, not because he once lived in a cabin, but because he got out of it.

Valentine's Day

Age is like love. It cannot be hidden.

The world needs more warm hearts and fewer hot heads.

You can always get someone to love you — even if you have to do it yourself.

Democracy, like love, can survive almost any attack — except neglect and indifference.

There would be fewer divorces if men gave as much loving attention to their wives as they do to their cars, boats, and dogs.

Love is the quest, marriage the conquest, divorce the inquest.

A dog is the only thing on earth that loves you more than he loves himself.

If dogs can think, how can we account for their love for man?

The fellow who is deeply in love with himself should get a divorce.

Love looks through a telescope; envy, through a microscope.

In the language of flowers, the yellow rose means friendship, the red rose means love, and the orchid means business.

Money can build a house, but it takes love to make it a home.

A house is made of walls and beams; a home is built with love and dreams.

Love is the glue that cements friendship; jealousy keeps it from sticking.

Kindness is the ability to love people more than they really deserve.

Kindness is the insignia of a loving heart.

To love and to labor is the sum of life; and, yet, how many think they are living when they neither love nor labor?

The most lonely place in the world is the human heart when love is absent.

Love at first sight may be all right, but it might be wise to take a second look.

To some people love is only the last word in a telegram.

Love is a little word; people make it big.

We are often told that love is blind — it can also be deaf and dumb.

Love makes a man think almost as much of a woman as he thinks of himself.

You can give without loving, but you can't love without giving.

Happiness is a healthy mental attitude, a grateful spirit, a clear conscience, and a heart full of love.

Happiness is the conviction that we are loved in spite of ourselves.

Service is nothing but love in work clothes.

You know a woman is in love with her husband if she smiles at him the way she does at a traffic cop.

What a nice world this world would be if we loved others as we love ourselves.

This will be a better world when the power of love replaces the love of power.

What kids need today is plenty of LSD — Love, Security, and Discipline.

If you had it all to do over, would you fall in love with yourself again?

Nothing beats love at first sight except love with insight.

A man doesn't know the value of a woman's love until he starts paying alimony.

Love is an unusual game. There are either two winners or none.

A husband knows his wife loves him when she returns a dress he can't afford.

To love the world is no big chore. It's that miserable guy next door who's the problem!

The way the cost of living and taxes are today, you might as well marry for love.

If love is blind, why are so many men attracted to a beautiful woman?

Love is the beautiful story, and marriage is the "talkie" version of it.

The biggest drawback to budding love these days is the *blooming* expense.

Love may make the world go 'round, but so will a big swallow of tobacco juice.

There are two sides to every question, except when it happens to be a love triangle.

The course of true love never runs — it stops and parks!

Love doesn't really make the world go round. It just makes people so dizzy it looks like it.

A girl may love you from the bottom of her heart, but there's always room for some other fellow at the top.

Love may be blind but it seems to find its way around.

A woman cherishes the memory of her first love affair with the same zeal with which a man forgets his.

Love is a condition of the mind at a time when the mind is out of condition.

Love is a fabric which never fades, no matter how often it is washed in the water of adversity and grief.

When you hear bells ringing, feel butterflies fluttering, and act as though you have bees in your bonnet — that's real love!

Love intoxicates a man; marriage often sobers him.

All the world loves a lover except when he is driving his automobile in crowded traffic — with his arm around his girlfriend.

It's hard to keep a man's love with cold food.

Love does not keep a ledger of the sins and failures of others.

Love is a ticklish sensation around the heart that can't be scratched!

The train of brotherly love rides on the track of concern and compassion.

Love your enemies. It'll sure make them feel foolish.

A woman feels a man's love should be like a toothbrush. It shouldn't be shared.

Mother love is dangerous when it becomes *smother* love.

Works, not words, are the proof of love.

It's useless to try to hold some people to anything they say while they're madly in love, drunk, or running for office.

The fellow who is too deeply in love with himself ought to get a divorce.

Love conquers all things except poverty and toothaches.

Don't underestimate love at first sight. Many of us might not pass a second inspection.

"Puppy love" is just a prelude to a dog's life.

A woman knows the value of love, but a man knows its cost.

The sunlight of love will kill all the germs of jealousy and hate.

Love is sharing a part of yourself with others.

First love is a little foolishness and a lot of curiosity.

The love of God cannot be merited or earned, but it can be spurned.

It is impossible to express love with a clenched fist.

Love is oceans of emotions surrounded by expanses of expenses.

The trouble with blind love is that it doesn't stay that way.

True love doesn't consist of holding hands — it consists of holding hearts.

The most important thing a father can do for his children is to love their mother.

It's easier to love humanity as a whole than to love one's neighbor.

Love covers a multitude of sins — temporarily.

Those who deserve love least need it most.

The Bible admonishes us to love our neighbors, and also to love our enemies — probably because they are generally the same people.

Of all human passions love is the strongest, for it attacks simultaneously the head, the heart, and the senses.

What silly things human beings utter when drunk or in love!

There are three things most men love but never understand: females, girls, and women.

Everything in the household runs smoothly when love oils the machinery.

Duty makes us do things well, but love makes us do them beautifully.

Love is like a vaccination — when it takes hold, you don't have to be told.

It probably would be all right if we'd love our neighbors as we love ourselves — but could they stand that much affection?

Love quickens all the senses — except common sense.

It would be a happy world if love were as easy to keep as it is to make.

Another good way for a young man to waste his breath is trying to be reasonable about love.

Love is more easily demonstrated than defined.

One of the tragedies of American life is that love is being defined by those who have experienced so little of it.

Love is the fairest flower that blooms in God's garden.

Love at first sight usually ends with divorce at first slight.

It's much wiser to love thy neighbor than his wife.

The course of true love never runs smoothly — and the detours aren't much better.

Love is something different from delirium, but it's hard to tell the difference.

To love others makes us happy; to love ourselves makes us lonely.

He loved a girl so much he worshiped the very ground her father discovered oil on.

Booze is the only enemy that man has succeeded in loving.

Love has been defined as something that makes a fellow feel funny and act foolish.

Love is a disease you can't "catch" without being properly exposed.

Illicit love isn't very much fun once it gets into court.

True love doesn't have a happy ending; true love doesn't have an ending.

Love is the only game in which two can play and both lose.

Love at first sight is often cured by a second look.

He who falls in love with himself will have no rivals.

Washington's Birthday

If George Washington never told a lie, what's his picture doing on a dollar bill that's worth about forty-three cents?

George Washington set a poor precedent when he threw that dollar across the Potomac. Since then our government has felt impelled to throw billions of them across the oceans.

Not only is Washington's face on our money, but now Washington's hands are on it.

George Washington never told a lie — but then he entered politics when the country was very young.

George Washington never told a lie, but then he never had to file a Form 1040.

Our country has made great progress. George Washington couldn't tell a lie. Now, just about everybody tells them.

If the dollar bill shrinks much more, George Washington will be forced to get a haircut.

Water pollution is getting worse each passing day. If George Washington were alive today he could roll that dollar across the Potomac.

George Washington was not a fisherman — he never told a lie!

George Washington was first in war, first in peace, and first to have his birthday juggled to make a long weekend.

George Washington could broadjump twenty-three feet, which was a record in those days. Today we have politicians who can sidestep farther than that.

It was easier to tell the truth in George Washington's day. There were no income-tax forms to fill out.

Lent

You deny Christ when you fail to deny yourself for Christ.

First give yourself to God, then giving your possessions will be easy and joyful.

He who reigns within himself, and rules passions, desires, and fears, is more than a king.

The concept of resurrection is welcomed by all; but the necessary, prior concern of self-crucifixion is a higher price than most people are willing to pay.

Many people have given up meat for Lent.
Others have given it up for rent.

> To search our souls
> To meditate
> Will not suffice
> For Lent.

> To share the cross,
> To sacrifice,
> These are the things
> God meant.

Jane McKay Lanning

March

Easter

The empty cross and the empty tomb speak of a full salvation.

Too many people mistake Easter Day for Decoration Day.

Big news of Easter: Jesus Christ is risen! Big question of Easter: Have you seen Him?

An empty tomb proves Christianity; an empty church denies it.

A great many young men are like Easter hats — mostly trimmings.

Many come to church to bring their new clothes rather than themselves.

April

Income Tax Day

Ambition in America is still rewarded — with high taxes.

America is a land of opportunity. Everybody can become a taxpayer.

America is the only country in the world where it takes more brains to make out the income tax return than it does to make the income.

There are two things in America that are growing bigger together — garbage cans and taxes.

It's hard to believe that America was founded to avoid high taxation.

Americans everywhere are now in a daze from INTAXICATION.

We often wonder if automation will ever replace the taxpayer!

There was a time when $200 was the down-payment on a car; now it's the sales tax.

There was a time when you saved up for your old age; now you save up for April 15th.

Every year around April 15 Americans have a rendezvous with debt.

There's no tax on brains; the take would be too small.

Business is tough these days. If a man does something wrong he gets fined; if he does something right he gets taxed.

An Oklahoma businessman reports that if his business gets any worse he won't have to lie on his next income-tax return.

Capital punishment is when Washington comes up with a new tax.

Capital punishment is when the government taxes you to get capital so that it can go into business in competition with you, and then taxes the profit on your business in order to pay its losses.

Drive carefully. Uncle Sam needs every taxpayer he can get.

Children may be deductible, but they're still taxing.

There's no child so bad that he can't be used as an income-tax deduction.

Nothing makes a man so modest about his income as a tax form to fill out.

17

Congress is confronted with the unsolved problem of how to get the people to pay taxes they can't afford for services they don't need.

We don't seem to be able to check crime, so why not legalize it and then tax it out of business?

One of the great blessings about living in a democracy is that we have complete control over how we pay our taxes — cash, check, or money order.

Ours is a democracy where the rich and the poor are alike — both complain about taxes.

The next disarmament conference might be a great success if the delegates were representative taxpayers.

The wealth of experience is one possession that has not yet been taxed.

A fool and his money are soon parted. The rest of us wait until income-tax time.

This country is as free today as it ever was — unless you happen to be a taxpayer.

Golf is a lot like taxes — you drive hard to get to the green and then wind up in the hole.

It's a mistake to believe that government can give things to some people without first taking it away from others.

Some folks feel the government owes them a living. The rest of us would gladly settle for a small tax refund.

One great thing about our form of government is that everybody gets something out of it, even if it's only free income-tax forms.

The government should supply a slide rule, prayerbook, and a Ouija Board with each income-tax form.

President Herbert Hoover was the first President to give his salary back to the government. Now the government would like everybody to do it.

Everybody works for the government, either on the payroll or the taxroll.

It seems that every time Congress sets out to trim the budget, the knife slips and trims the taxpayers instead.

Even if money could buy happiness, just think what a luxury tax there'd be!

A man's home is his castle. At least that's how it seems when he pays taxes on it.

The honeymoon is over when the bride begins to suspect that she was never anything to him but a tax deduction.

Don't you long for the "good old days" when Uncle Sam lived within his income and without most of yours?

Pity the guy in the middle-income bracket — earning too much to avoid paying taxes, and not enough to afford paying taxes.

Our income-tax forms this year have been simplified beyond all understanding.

Most of us secretly wish we were so rich that we wouldn't have to pay an income tax.

In preparing his income-tax return, the average American man resembles a girl getting ready to go to the beach. They both take off as much as the law allows.

Wouldn't it be great if we could force the recall of all Form 1040s?

It's strange how a man with no sense of humor can come up with such funny answers on his income-tax returns!

The reason they say the income tax is the fairest tax of all is that it gives every individual an even chance at poverty.

When making out your income-tax returns, 'it's better to give than to deceive.'

They tell us they are going to do something about junk mail, but they continue to send out income-tax forms.

When it comes to income tax, most of us would be willing to pay as we go if we could only catch up on where we've been.

An income-tax return is like a girdle. If you put the wrong figure in it, you're apt to get pinched.

The attitude of Congress toward hidden taxes is not to do away with them, but to hide them better.

After a man pays his income tax, he knows how a cow feels after she's been milked.

The latest income-tax form has been greatly simplified. It consists of only three parts: (1) How much did you make last year? (2) How much have you got left? (3) Send amount listed in part 2.

It is generally agreed that the income tax is the government's idea of instant poverty.

Next to being shot at and missed, nothing is quite as satisfactory as an income-tax refund.

An income-tax form is like a laundry list — either way you lose your shirt.

About the time a man is cured of swearing, another income tax is due.

When they consider candidates for the next Pulitzer Prize for the best definitive biography, many a man would be delighted to submit his last income-tax report.

Loafing is the only way to beat the income tax.

Nothing has done more to stimulate the writing of fiction than the itemized deduction section of the income-tax forms.

The income tax has made more liars out of the American people than golf.

People who squawk about their income tax can be divided into two classes: men and women.

If you want to get even with the income-tax people, get Junior to work out your tax return using the new math.

The average man knows as much about the atomic bomb as he does about his income-tax form.

Income taxes are not so bad and certainly could be worse. Suppose we had to pay on what we think we are worth?

What the present income-tax form needs is a section which would explain the explanations.

When making out your income-tax report, be sure you don't overlook your most expensive dependent — the government.

Income-tax forms are nothing more than the government's quiz program.

Some of us can recall the day when a person who had to pay income tax was considered to be wealthy.

No stretch of the imagination is as complete as the one used in filling out income-tax forms.

Income tax is the fine you pay for thriving so fast.

It is difficult to predict the future of an economy in which it takes more brains to figure out the tax on our income than it does to earn it.

Income-tax forms should be printed on Kleenex because so many of us have to pay through the nose.

We wouldn't mind paying income tax if we could know which country it's going to.

Income-tax forms should be more realistic by allowing the taxpayer to list Uncle Sam as a dependent.

Paying your income tax is for a good cause — such as keeping you out of the penitentiary.

In 1913 Uncle Sam collected only 13 million dollars in income taxes. That's why they were called the "good old days."

The guy who said that truth never hurts never had to fill out a Form 1040.

Come to think of it, these income-tax forms leave little to the imagination and even less to the taxpayer.

Just thinking about income taxes often taxes the mind — which is something people once said the IRS couldn't do.

Trying to curb inflation by raising taxes is like giving a drunk another drink to sober him up.

If you think you can keep everything to yourself, the IRS doesn't.

If the IRS gave green stamps, thousands of Americans would look forward to paying their income tax.

With a billion dollar budget, it ought to be possible to set aside enough money to teach the IRS the basic English necessary to write a readable income-tax form.

Another American invention is the permanent temporary tax.

There are no curse words in the Indian language. They don't need any because they don't pay taxes.

The best tax law is the one that gets the most feathers with the least squawking.

Which has made the biggest liars out of Americans — golf or the income tax?

A man in Oklahoma admitted he lied on his income-tax return — he listed himself as the head of the household!

Life is one dodge after another — cars, taxes, and responsibilities.

The best things in life are free — plus tax, of course.

The way the cost of living and taxes are today, you might as well marry for love.

The average man now lives thirty-one years longer than he did in 1850. He has to in order to get his taxes paid.

A serious impediment to a successful marriage these days is the difficulty of supporting both the government and a wife on one small income.

Blessed are the meek for they shall inherit the earth — less 40 percent inheritance tax.

When the time comes for the meek to inherit the earth, taxes will most likely be so high that they won't want it.

The meek may inherit the earth just in time to see it sold for taxes.

Of course you can't take it with you, and with high taxes, lawyer's fees, and funeral expenses you can't leave it behind either.

Benjamin Franklin had an axiom, "A penny saved is a penny earned." But that was before the sales tax was invented.

A lot of people still have the first dollar they ever made — Uncle Sam has all the others.

A harp is a piano after taxes.

We need to change our National Anthem to "Deep in the Heart of Taxes."

A good name is to be chosen over great riches. It's tax free!

No respectable person is in favor of nudity, but after paying taxes, some of us may not have any other choice.

What this country needs most is a SPCT — The Society for the Prevention of Cruelty to Taxpayers.

Patriotism will probably never develop to the point of parading in honor of the "unknown taxpayer."

A dyed-in-the-wool patriot is one who says he's sorry he has only one income to give to his country.

Wouldn't it be grand if politicians would fight poverty with something besides taxes?

After all is said and done, the politicians say it and the taxpayers do it.

It is reported that the politicians in Washington are thinking of abolishing the income tax — and taking the income.

Regardless of who wins the election they have to raise taxes to pay for the damage.

If our President wants to abolish poverty, he can do it by abolishing the IRS.

Poverty is what you experience the day after you pay your income tax.

One of the biggest advantages of being poor is that you'll never have to undergo the trauma of a tax audit.

The chaplains who pray for the United States Senate and the House of Representatives might speak a word now and then on behalf of the taxpayers.

Unquestionably, there is progress everywhere. The average American now pays out as much in taxes as he formerly received in wages.

Our beloved country has made remarkable progress. Now politicians have arranged to spend taxes before they collect them.

A political promise today means another tax tomorrow.

We may need tax reform, but it seems we need a lot of spending reform too.

The futility of riches is stated very plainly in two places: the Bible and the income-tax form.

In Russia the people have only what the government gives them; in America the people have only what the government does not take away from them in taxes.

If science says nothing is impossible, how about a mechanical taxpayer?

Science has increased our life span considerably. Now we can look forward to paying our taxes at least ten years longer.

Space scientists have made an analysis of the lunar soil. It shows that corn can't be raised on the moon, but it's great for raising taxes.

At no time is it easier to keep your mouth shut than during an audit of your income-tax return.

Our government could raise unlimited revenue simply by taxing sin.

Being a success today means the government takes away in taxes what you used to dream of earning.

An American can consider himself a success when it costs him more to support the government than to support a wife and children.

Patrick Henry ought to come back and see what taxation *with* representation is like.

Taxation, like a lot of other things, is based on supply and demand. The government demands, we supply.

The greatest general to emerge from any war is general taxation.

Taxation is the gentle art of picking the goose in such a way as to secure the greatest amount of feathers with the least amount of squawking.

Taxation is a lot like sheep shearing. As long as you shear a sheep it will continue to produce a new crop of wool. But you can skin the animal only once.

If something new has been added, it's probably another tax.

The man who said taxes would keep us halfway broke was a lousy judge of distance.

The only thing left to tax is the wolf at the door.

Why don't high taxes and high prices marry and settle down?

Is there any human activity that isn't taxed, licensed, regulated, or restricted?

It looks like we all will eventually make our living collecting taxes from one another.

Stay on your job and pay your taxes promptly. Thousands of workers in the government bureaus are counting on you.

A penny saved is a penny taxed.

There is nothing more permanent than a temporary tax.

When it comes to a tax reduction, never has so little been waited for by so many for so long.

Why not slap a tax on political gas?

After paying all our taxes we're tempted to call Washington and try to get ourselves declared a disaster area.

Another difference between death and taxes is that death is frequently painless.

Tax forms are entirely too complicated and get worse every year. All they have to do is "simplify" them one more time and nobody will be able to understand them.

You really can't beat the game. If you win anything, it's minus taxes. If you buy anything, it's plus taxes.

The tobacco industry would really be doing something if it could come up with a cigarette that eliminated tar, nicotine, and taxes.

The path of civilization is paved with tax receipts.

One hopeful note on hidden taxes is that there can't be many more places to hide them.

We wonder why they call them "tax returns" when so little of it does.

The best things in life are still free, but the tax experts are working overtime on the problem.

We all get excited these days about paying taxes because we never know which country our money is going to.

It will be real nice if taxes get down to where we can afford to make a living.

What's all this howling about hidden taxes? We wish they would hide all of them.

Next year will be the year they lower taxes — it always is.

Breathing seems to be about the only activity in this country that isn't taxed.

It's about time that somebody invents a tax that can't be hiked.

There's a "tax cocktail" on the market — two drinks and you withhold nothing.

A gentleman in Maryland says he's going to invest his money in taxes — the only sure thing to go up.

Old taxes never die — they just change their names.

A window sign in Chicago: "Tax Returns Prepared — Honest Mistakes Are Our Specialty."

Nowadays anybody who puts two and two together also has to add in the sales tax.

About the only thing about those withholding taxes is that a fellow doesn't get so mad all at once.

Increasing taxes to stop inflation makes about as much sense as fanning a fire to cool its heat.

A "slight tax increase" costs you about $300, while a "substantial tax cut" lowers your taxes by about $30.

A politician will consider every way of reducing taxes except cutting expenses.

When Congress tries to decide between two new taxes, it's like a woman deciding between two dresses — she usually decides to take both.

If you don't hear some people murmuring about taxes these days, it's probably because so many others are screaming.

Nobody jumps on taxes when they're down.

By the time you finish paying all your taxes, about all you have left is a receipt.

If Congress would repeal the nuisance tax, we wouldn't have any taxes to pay.

They keep telling us about a tax-freeze plan. How about a tax-free plan?

One can be born free and then be taxed to death.

The attitude of Congress toward hidden taxes is not to do away with them, but to hide them better.

When the average man looks at what he has left after his taxes are paid, he begins to realize that Social Security may have real meaning for him.

No matter how staggering the taxes, they never fall down.

When the time comes for the meek to inherit the earth, taxes will be so high they won't want it.

Save your pennies and the sales tax will take care of them.

Whenever one tax goes down, another goes up.

A certain Senator recently informed us that the average American is not "tax conscious," and this is doubtless true. If he shows signs of coming to, he is immediately struck down with another tax.

There's one consolation about life and taxes — when you finish the former, you're through with the latter.

We have been anesthetized by hidden taxes, hypnotized by indirect taxes, and pulverized by camouflaged taxes.

Nothing is certain in this world except death, taxes, and teen-agers.

The reward for saving your money is being able to pay your taxes without borrowing.

A tax-dodger is a man who does not love his country less, but loves his money more.

Everything we have is taxed — even our patience.

Thinking is one thing that no one has ever been able to tax — but the IRS is getting jealous about the situation.

"What you don't know doesn't hurt you" doesn't apply to the hidden taxes in the things you buy.

A man pays a luxury tax on a leather billfold, an income tax on the stuff he puts into it, and a sales tax when he takes the stuffing out of it.

Take a look at your tax bills and you'll quit calling them "cheap politicians."

It's a mistake to believe that Uncle Sam can open his pocketbook and let you keep yours closed.

The real patriot is a person who saves enough of his salary each week to pay his income tax.

A politician is a man who never met a tax he didn't try to hike.

A tax cut is like motherhood, apple pie, and the Star-Spangled Banner — everybody is for it.

We wouldn't mind this "pay-as-you-go" tax so much if we knew what we were paying for and where it was going.

If taxes climb any higher, they may go into orbit.

A man listed the government as a dependent on his income-tax return. The claim was disallowed because he wasn't contributing more than one half of his income toward its support.

There doesn't seem to be any justice. If you fill out an income-tax return correctly, you go to the poorhouse. If you don't, you go to jail.

A tax refund is the next best thing to being shot at and missed.

Have you noticed that everytime something terrible happens any place in the world, someone in Washington tries to use it as an excuse to raise taxes?

Let's be thankful we don't have to pay taxes on our debts.

A tax cut is the 'kindest cut of all.'

New taxes are like mustard plasters — easy to put on but almost impossible to remove.

Most of us have enough money to pay our taxes. What we need is something to live on!

The fellow who said "What goes up must come down" must have lived before they invented taxes and postal rates.

There's no tax on brains — the take would be too small.

With taxes what they are today, a fellow has to be unemployed to make a living.

The tax-eaters are destroying the tax-earners.

Taxes and politicians are closely related. Once we get stuck with a tax, the only thing politicians know how to do is to raise it.

Some tax refunds are slower than a helicopter over a nudist colony.

The thing raised most abundantly in the United States is taxes.

Those who think their tax dollars don't go very far should glance at the moon occasionally.

Actually we wouldn't mind Uncle Sam's tax bite — if he didn't come back for dessert.

As we pay our taxes, most of us are not worried about Congress letting us down — but we often wonder if it will ever let us up.

Responsibility for a considerable portion of the world's troubles rests upon two people of the past. One of them invented credit; the other, taxes.

The trouble with today's taxes is that they keep your take-home pay from ever getting there.

Nothing has done more to stimulate the writing of fiction than the itemized deduction on the income-tax form.

The income tax, the property tax, and the sales tax are an unbeatable combination. They get you coming and going. Add the inheritance tax and they get you after you've gone.

With estate taxes what they are, the happiest mourner at a rich man's funeral is Uncle Sam.

People who grumble about taxes have one consolation — they don't have to pay on what they think they're worth.

The way taxes are now, you seldom hear any more about a girl getting married for money.

Tax collectors are funny folks. They expect a fellow to give them the money he's already spent for something better.

With another tax hike pants pockets will become unnecessary.

It's getting so your annual property tax is more than you paid for your home in the first place.

Regardless of who wins the election they'll raise your taxes to pay for the damage.

What about welfare for the taxpayer? He isn't faring so well these days either!

There should be a special watch for the taxpayer — it wouldn't tick, just wring its hands.

A California taxpayer recently moaned, "I owe the government so much money it doesn't know whether to throw me out or recognize me as a foreign power."

Taxpayers are always hoping for a break in the levy.

The only thing easier to skin than a banana is a taxpayer.

Regardless of where a shot is fired in the world today, the American taxpayer is the one who is invariably hit.

When taxpayers go broke or crazy, or both, they are taken care of by those who haven't gone yet.

Pound for pound the American taxpayer is the strongest creature on earth. For many years he has been carrying Washington and a considerable portion of the world on his shoulders.

A taxpayer recently sent the IRS twenty-five cents with a note saying he understood that he could pay his taxes by the quarter.

The trouble with our foreign policy is that the enemy nations are living beyond our means.

The only people who don't have to pass the Civil Service exams to work for the government are taxpayers.

If the folks in Washington are so disturbed about human suffering, they ought to take a look at the American taxpayer.

It has been suggested that we have a new postage stamp bearing the picture of a weeping taxpayer.

The president has the next to the hardest job in the United States. The taxpayer has the hardest.

It's a lot easier to trim the taxpayer than to trim the budget.

The elephant and the donkey were probably chosen as political party emblems because they are beasts of burden. If a new political party is started, a taxpayer might suitably be used as an emblem.

A deputy income-tax collector in Washington was recently the victim of a holdup man who took all his money and stripped him to his underwear. Now he knows how we taxpayers feel.

It takes the wool of twenty sheep and the hides of ten taxpayers to clothe one United States soldier.

The American taxpayers wouldn't object to free transportation for certain government officials if they'd go where we wish they would.

A taxpayer resents the fact that death and taxes don't come in that order!

Trimming expenses in government operations is the last resort when the taxpayers can stand no more trimming.

A taxpayer might be referred to as a government worker with no vacations, no sick leaves, and no holidays.

It seems that almost every group of workers now has a union except taxpayers.

Flying saucers are nothing but taxpayers blowing their tops.

Instead of taking the pants off the taxpayer it might be better to take the vest off the vested interests.

After the government takes enough to balance the budget, the taxpayer has the job of budgeting the balance.

Any company that manufactures a mechanical taxpayer will make a fortune in a hurry!

Taxpayers are the casualties of the War on Poverty.

It might be well to bear in mind that when Uncle Sam plays Santa Claus, it's the taxpayer who holds the bag.

We should not become too enthusiastic until some statesman comes along with a scheme to make the world perfect without soaking the taxpayer.

In the near future Congress is expected to raise the legal limit on the taxpayer's patience.

We've had the New Deal and the Fair Deal. Some taxpayers are calling what we have now the Ordeal.

What Americans need most is "Taxicare" to help us pay our taxes.

Nowadays many taxpayers are writing letters of protest to their congressmen — and some are so hot they're steaming themselves open.

If Washington D. C. is the seat of government, then the taxpayer is the pants pocket.

Most American taxpayers gladly support their own government by paying their taxes promptly, but they resent having to support the government of several other countries.

Nothing spurs a taxpayer into filing an income-tax return like the expectation of a refund.

They say politics makes strange bedfellows, but it's the taxpayer who has the nightmare.

It seems like a lot of taxpayers are suffering from "shell-out shock."

In the old days it was two chickens in every pot; now it's two government employees for every taxpayer.

Any government big enough to give you everything you want is big enough to take everything you've got.

No enemy nation could risk invading the United States. It couldn't afford the high taxes.

In view of the inheritance tax, the meek and humble will get nothing when they inherit the earth.

Some tax loopholes become nooses.

Death and taxes are inevitable, but death is not a repeater.

When all is said and done, it's the politicians who say it and the taxpayers who do it.

The taxpayer who thinks his money doesn't go very far should brush up on his geography.

It appears that Congress has found it's a lot easier to trim the taxpayers than expenses.

Congress does some strange things — it puts a high tax on liquor, and raises the other taxes that drive people to drink.

The biggest job Congress has is how to get money from the taxpayers without disturbing the voters.

Making out your own income-tax return is something like a do-it-yourself mugging.

Three cases where supply exceeds demand are: taxes, trouble, and advice.

The ideal form of taxation is the kind that will be paid by somebody else.

Our forefathers should have fought for representation without taxation!

The new income-tax form is printed in red, white, and blue. When you've filled in the white, you're left in the red, and that makes you blue.

The shorter the time to April 15, the longer the face of the taxpayer.

With all the hidden taxes, what about a place where the taxpayer can hide?

The American taxpayer is the unforgotten man.

This talk about a "new source of revenue" simply means tapping the same old taxpayer in a brand new place.

It's getting to where even the taxpayer's patience is being taxed.

Pity the poor taxpayer who has the whole government on his payroll.

There's nothing wrong with teen-agers that becoming taxpayers won't cure.

We often wondered why Uncle Sam wears such a tall hat, until he started passing it around for taxes.

It often seems like the United States is building up its enemies and flattening its taxpayers.

Advice to vacationers: Don't overtax yourself. The government will do it for you.

The two agencies now being used to redistribute wealth are taxation and offspring.

Untold wealth is the wealth which does not appear on income-tax returns.

Nowadays when you miss a day's work the government loses as much as you do.

A person doesn't realize how much he has to be thankful for until he has to pay taxes on it.

It was easier to tell the truth in George Washington's day. There were no income-tax forms to fill out.

Behind every successful man stands a woman and the IRS. One takes the credit, and the other takes the cash.

Nowadays the world revolves on its taxes.

Income tax is Uncle Sam's version of "Truth or Consequences."

Only two kinds of people complain about excessive taxes — men and women.

One thing about death — it doesn't get worse every time Congress meets.

It has almost reached the point where, if a person takes a day off, he falls behind in his income-tax payments.

A dime is a dollar with all the various taxes deducted.

The reward for saving money is being able to pay our taxes without borrowing.

A father in Georgia called his local IRS office to ask if he could deduct the cost of his daughter's wedding as a "total loss"?

The sneakiest two words in the English language are "plus tax."

Secretary's Day

You may know more than your employer, but his knowledge pays off.

A certain boss said to his secretary, "Congratulations! This is the earliest you've been late in a long time."

Before arguing with your boss, make absolutely sure you're right — then let the matter drop.

Retirement is when your wife realizes she never gave your secretary enough sympathy.

Nothing is quite as embarrassing as watching your boss do something you assured him couldn't be done.

The best way to appreciate your job is to imagine yourself without one.

Computers will never replace human beings entirely. Someone has to complain about the errors.

You'll find that the big potatoes are on top of the heap because there are a lot of little potatoes holding them up.

Before you have an argument with your boss, you'd better take a good look at both sides — his side and the outside.

Ulcers are contagious. You can get them from your boss.

The hardest job in the world is telling the boss the computer proved him wrong.

Being diplomatic is telling your boss he has an open mind instead of telling him he has a hole in the head.

May

Mother's Day

A mother takes twenty-one years to make a man of her boy, and another woman can make a fool of him in twenty minutes.

There are still a few old-fashioned mothers who would like to tuck their children in bed, but they can't stay awake that late.

The most difficult thing for a mother to remember is that other people have perfect children too.

A mother is a woman who decorates her life with babies.

It has been rightly said that a mother is not a person to lean on, but a person to make leaning unnecessary.

We are now told that automation is a process that gets all the work done while you just stand there. When we were younger, this process was called MOTHER.

The most terrible thing about a divorce is that somewhere, maybe miles apart, two mothers are nodding their heads and saying, "See? I told you so."

Mother love is dangerous when it becomes *smother* love.

Rejecting things because they are old-fashioned would rule out the sun and the moon — and a mother's love.

Many a man met his wife through a dating service — her mother!

A modern mother is one who worries only when her daughter gets home from a date at a decent hour.

A mother's patience is like a tube of toothpaste — it's never quite all gone.

There's only one perfect child in the world and every mother has it.

The joys of motherhood are never fully experienced until all the children are in bed.

What a mother should save for a rainy day is patience.

A mother in Colorado is so ashamed of her unruly kids that she attends the PTA under an assumed name.

Have you ever wondered what some mothers would find to talk about if their children weren't allergic to something?

You can be sure it's her firstborn if a mother cries when Junior starts school.

29

A man is seldom as smart as his mother thinks, or as dumb as his mother-in-law says he is.

A mother who makes a match for her daughter usually intends to referee it as well.

A mother may hope that her daughter will get a better husband than she did, but she knows her son will never get as good a wife as his father did.

Another reason for unhappy marriages is that men can't fool their wives like they could their mothers.

All mothers are physically handicapped. They have only two hands.

A mother should be like a quilt — keep the children warm but don't smother them.

The old-fashioned mother who used to have prunes every morning now has a granddaughter who has dates every night.

Most mothers aren't really interested in taking their weight off — they just want to rearrange it.

The mother of the bride gushed, "I hope she'll make *her* husband as happy as she's making *my* husband."

Simply having children does not necessarily make a woman a mother.

A modern mother is one who can hold a safety pin and a cigarette in her mouth at the same time.

Mothers can have a few minutes to themselves at the end of the day by doing the dishes.

The young mother gets along beautifully with her mother-in-law because she probably can't afford a baby sitter.

A Mississippi mother said to her children, "Mind your manners, they may come back in style someday."

It took the old-time mother less than a minute to dress for dinner. All she had to do was take off her apron.

Many mothers had their daughters vaccinated in places they wrongly thought would never show.

Mothers who scold their sons for carrying useless things in their pockets should take a look in their handbags!

On the matrimonial sea, the hand that rocks the cradle seldom rocks the boat.

Throughout the ages no nation has ever had a better friend than the mother who taught her children to pray.

Why does a mother do all she can to help her daughter catch a man — and then cry at her wedding?

The quickest way for a mother to get her children's attention is to sit down and look comfortable.

A typical mother, seeing there are only four pieces of pie for five people, promptly announces she never did care for pie.

Memorial Day

Washington has a large assortment of peace monuments. They build one after every war.

War does not determine who is right — only who is left. Next time it won't even do that.

Old men declare wars, but it is youth that must fight them.

The highest honor that could be paid to the "Unknown Soldier" would be to not have any more of them in the future.

As we bargain for peace let us remember there will be no refunds on lives given toward the same purpose.

History shows that war is better at abolishing nations than nations are at abolishing war.

General Sherman defined war as hell, but the definition of a modern peace is unprintable.

Even peace may be purchased at too high a price.

War does not, and cannot, prove which side is right, but only which side is stronger.

The tragedy of war is that it uses man's best to do man's worst.

It seems that perfect peace can be found only in the cemetery.

June

Flag Day

An American and a Dutchman were talking. "What does your flag look like?" asked the American. "It has 3 stripes," replied the Dutchman, "red, white and blue. We say they have a connection with our taxes: we get red when we talk about them, white when we get our tax bills, and we pay 'til we're blue in the face."

"That's just how it is here," commented the American, "only we see stars, too."

Some people *wave* the American flag but *waive* what it stands for.

Father's Day

Education is something you get when your father sends you to college, but it isn't complete until you send your own son.

The extravagant girl usually makes a poor mother and a bankrupt father.

The parents gave their daughter a new car as a birthday present. On the windshield was a card signed, "With all our love. Mama and Pauper."

The trouble with the average juvenile delinquent is not always apparent — sometimes it's two parents!

Juvenile delinquency is no mystery. Mama is so busy keeping up with the Joneses and Papa is so busy keeping up with Mama that neither of them has any time left for keeping up with John and Mary.

Christmas shopping should include buying toys for the children that their father would enjoy playing with.

A father who encourages his boy to follow in his footsteps has probably forgotten a few.

Children always know when company is in the living room — they can hear their mother laughing at their father's jokes.

College debts are obligations that with diligence, economy, and stern self-denial, father will be able to pay.

A diplomat is a parent with two boys on different Little League teams.

It used to be when a boy couldn't learn at his mother's knee he found himself over his father's.

Did you hear about the father who fainted when his son asked for the keys to the garage and came out with the lawn mower?

Many modern dads worry more about their golf swing than they do their offspring.

A Kentucky father of a teen-age boy says his hardest job is getting his son to realize that "No" is a complete sentence.

A father in Georgia called his local IRS office to ask if he could deduct the cost of his daughter's wedding as a "total loss"?

A father expects his son to be as good as he meant to be.

After paying for the wedding, about the only thing a father has left to give away is the bride.

The most important thing a father can do for his children is to love their mother.

A real family man is one who looks at his new child as an addition rather than a deduction.

A distressed father said to his teen-age daughter, "Young lady, either that dress is too short or you're not in it far enough."

In the old days a father didn't have to take his kid to a psychiatrist to find out that he was a little stinker.

A father is usually more pleased to have his child look like him than act like him.

Father must work for two reasons: Christmas and vacation.

Mother to father about their rebellious son, "And to think we planned him."

A father is often a man who is working his son's way through college.

Every father should remember that one day his son will follow his example instead of his advice.

The modern father wants his son to have all the things he never had — such as straight A's on his report card.

The average father is one who wears out a pair of shoes while the rest of the family wears out a set of tires.

Children's Day

The guy whose troubles are all behind him is probably a school bus driver.

The child who knows the value of a dollar these days must be terribly discouraged.

The trouble with teaching a child the value of a dollar is you have to do it almost every week.

Every child comes into the world endowed with liberty, opportunity, and a share of the war debt.

The two agencies now being used to redistribute wealth are taxation and offspring.

Things are pretty well evened up in this world. Other people's troubles are not as bad as ours, but their children are a lot worse.

It's hard, if not impossible, to get a child to pay attention to you, especially when you're telling him something for his own good.

Some adolescents become bad eggs because they have been set on too long — or not long enough.

Never strike a child! You might miss and hurt yourself.

Some kids are like ketchup bottles. You have to slap their bottoms a few times to get them moving.

All children don't disobey their parents. Some are never told what to do.

The child who always complains he's getting the short end of the stick should be given more of it.

Some children grow like weeds and are about as well cared for.

Children brought up in Sunday school are seldom brought up in court.

There are many "bright children" who should be applauded with one hand.

One important way for us to help our children grow up is for us to grow up first.

There are still a few people who can remember when a child misbehaved to get attention — and got it!

Spoiled kids soon become little stinkers.

If brushing up on manners doesn't help some children, the brush should be moved down a bit.

One advantage of the compact car is that when any of the kids start acting up they can be reached by hand.

The behavior of some children suggests that their parents embarked on the sea of matrimony without a paddle.

A boy loves a dog because it's the only thing around the house that doesn't find fault with him.

One way to keep young boys from getting on the wrong track is to use better switching facilities.

A pat on the back will develop character if given young enough, often enough, low enough — and hard enough.

Some of today's children don't smart in the right place.

Rearing children is the biggest "heir-conditioning" job ever undertaken.

Psychiatry has certainly changed things. The kid who used to be just a chatterbox is now a "compulsive talker."

It's incredible when we think how little our parents knew about child psychology and how wonderful we turned out to be!

Child psychology is what children manage their parents with.

Where do kids get all those questions parents can't answer?

Efficient school teachers may cost more, but poor school teachers cost the most.

A teacher's constant task is to take a roomful of live wires and see to it that they're grounded.

Nothing improves a television program as much as getting the children to bed.

Children who watch television every night will go down in history — not to mention arithmetic, geography, and science.

You don't know what trouble is until your kids reach the age of consent, dissent, and resent — all at the same time.

Many children have grown up to be fairly levelheaded because their parents couldn't find the guidance book they were looking for.

Nowadays children are called bright when they make remarks that used to call for a good spanking.

When children get on the wrong track it's time to use the switch.

Child training is chiefly a matter of knowing which end of the child to pat — and when.

Training a child to follow the straight and narrow way is easy for parents — all they have to do is lead the way.

In bringing up children it's best not to let them know it.

Sometimes the best way to straighten out a child is by bending him over.

You have to give American parents credit — they know how to obey their children.

People who say they sleep like a baby haven't got one.

There's only one perfect child in the world and every mother has it.

A good way for your daughter to be popular is for you to be rich.

A major problem facing housewives is that ovens are self-cleaning but kids aren't.

Little Junior brought home what is now remembered as his Watergate report card. First, he denied there was one; then he couldn't find it. When he finally located it, three grades had been erased.

The hardest people to convince that they're ready to retire are children at bedtime.

If your youngster asks how Santa Claus gets into your house, tell him he comes in through a hole in daddy's wallet.

It's invariably the little devil in your neighborhood who starts the fight with your little angel.

Sleep is something that science cannot abolish — but babies can.

Never slap a child in the face. Remember, there's a *place* for everything.

It is extremely difficult to train a boy in the way his father does not go.

If a child annoys you, quiet him by brushing his hair — if this doesn't work, use the other side of the brush on the other end of the child.

It's better to teach children the roots of labor than to hand them the fruits of yours.

Theories on how to rear children usually end with the birth of the second child.

Every child has a right to be both well-fed and well-led.

To train children at home, it's necessary for both the children and the parents to spend some time there.

Someone has defined spanking as "stern" punishment.

The surest way to make it hard for your children is to make it soft for them.

You train a child until age ten; after that you only influence him.

Train your child in the way you now know you should have gone yourself.

The best way to bring up children is never to let them down.

Teaching children to count is not as important as teaching them *what* counts.

Another thing a modern child learns at his mother's knee is to watch out for cigarette ashes.

A switch in time saves crime.

Psychiatrists tell us that discipline doesn't break a child's spirit half as often as the lack of it breaks a parent's heart.

Discipline is what you inflict on one end of a child to impress the other.

By the time some parents get around to putting a foot down, the child already has his on the accelerator.

One of the problems of juvenile delinquency is children running away from home. It is entirely possible they may be looking for their parents.

Most juvenile delinquents are youngsters who have been given a free hand, but not in the proper place.

In the days when a woodshed stood behind the American home, a great deal of what passes as juvenile delinquency was settled out of court.

When a youth begins to sow wild oats it's time for father to start the threshing machine.

Juvenile delinquency is the result of parents trying to train their children without starting at the bottom.

Juvenile delinquency was unheard of many years ago because the problem was thrashed-out in the woodshed.

Did the conversion of so many woodsheds into garages have anything to do with the alarming increase in juvenile delinquency.?

The man who remembers what he learned at his mother's knee was probably bent over at the time.

A mother should be like a quilt — keep the children warm but don't smother them.

The time to teach obedience to authority is in the playpen instead of the State pen.

Too many parents tie up their dogs and allow their children to run loose.

The ability to say no is perhaps the greatest gift a parent has.

Some parents begin with giving in and end with giving up.

Some parents bring their children up, others let them down.

Judging by what we read in the papers, the reason some parents "spare the rod" is because Junior is carrying one.

A boy is like a canoe — he behaves better if paddled from the rear.

Nothing creates a firmer belief in heredity than having a good-looking child.

Home is a man's refuge, a place of quiet and rest, says a certain writer. That's true except for the telephone, the children, the vacuum cleaner, and the salesman at the door.

The honeymoon is definitely over when all the babytalk around the house is done only by the baby.

If you plan to teach your children the value of a dollar, you'll have to do it awfully fast.

A much-needed invention for the American scene is an automatic childwasher.

We need tougher child abuse laws — parents have taken enough abuse from their children.

A real family man is one who looks at his new child as an addition rather than a deduction.

Children often hold a marriage together by keeping their parents so busy they don't have time to quarrel.

A "miracle drug" is any medicine you can get the kids to take without screaming.

Another reason men don't live as long as women is that they suffer so much waiting around in hospitals for their wives to have babies.

A mother in Colorado is so ashamed of her unruly kids that she attends the PTA under an assumed name.

There are still a few old-fashioned mothers who would like to tuck their children in bed, but they can't stay awake that late.

When it comes to music lessons, most kids make it a practice not to practice.

Who said kids aren't obedient? They'll obey any TV commercial about buying a new toy.

You are quite old if you can remember when children were strong enough to walk to school.

When all the kids have grown up, married, and moved away, many parents experience a strange new emotion; it's called ecstacy.

All a parent has to do to make a child thirsty is to fall asleep.

Parents would not have to worry so much about how a kid turns out if they worried more about when he turns in.

Applied child psychology was more effective when the applicator was a small razor strap.

We've given our youngsters too much too soon, and now it's too late.

A typical home is where the TV set is better adjusted than the kids.

One reason for juvenile delinquency is that many parents are raising their children by remote control.

Any child who gets raised strictly by the book is probably a first edition.

A modern home is a place where a switch controls everything but the children.

Nothing lengthens the life of your car like marrying-off the last of your children.

A baby sitter is not experienced until she knows which kid to sit with and which kid to sit on.

A baby sitter is a teen-ager you hire to let your children do whatever they are big enough to do.

Most of us want other people's children to behave the way ours should.

Teachers in the lower grades needn't worry about automation until someone invents a machine that can blow noses and remove snowsuits and boots.

What the average man wants to get out of his new car is the kids.

Children are a great deal more apt to follow your lead than the way you point.

There are still a few people who can remember when a child misbehaved to get attention — and got it!

The easiest way to get a kid's attention is to stand in front of the TV set.

There's nothing thirstier than a child who has just gone to bed.

More children are spoiled because the parents won't spank Grandma.

A "brat" is a child who acts like your own but belongs to your neighbor.

Most children seldom misquote you; they repeat what you shouldn't have said word for word.

We can't understand why today's children are complaining so much. They're not old enough to remember what prices used to be.

Among the best home furnishings are children.

Infant care is another thing that has to be learned from the bottom up.

Many children would take after their parents if they knew where they went.

The best time to put kids to bed is very late — when they're too tired to fight back.

Little Willie is at the awkward age — too young to leave him home alone, and too old to trust with baby sitters.

Children always know when company is in the living room — they can hear their mother laughing at their father's jokes.

It's very difficult to teach children the alphabet these days. They think V comes right after T.

Children are so tough in big cities they no longer use bunnies for Easter — they use porcupines.

Parents are embarrassed when their children tell lies, but sometimes it's even worse when they tell the truth.

A child's definition of a torture chamber is a living room or den without a TV set.

If the church neglects the children, it is certain the children will neglect the church.

Cleanliness may be next to godliness, but in childhood it's next to impossible.

With the world in such a confused state, no wonder babies cry when they come into it.

Most kids think a balanced diet is a hamburger in each hand.

Every father should remember that one day his son will follow his example instead of his advice.

A great many children face the hard problem of learning good table manners without seeing any.

We learn from experience. A man never wakes up his second baby just to see it smile.

In some families it would be best if the children were properly spaced — about one hundred yards apart.

The advantage of a large family is that at least one of the children may not turn out like the others.

As the gardener is responsible for the products of his garden, so the family is responsible for the character and conduct of its children.

Families with babies and families without babies are sorry for each other.

Every part of the family constitutes a part of the family tree. Father is the rough bark and fiber, the rugged part which supports and protects it. Mother is the heart, which must be sound and true or the tree will die. The daughter may be likened to the leaves and flowers that adorn it. The son is almost always the sap.

A lucky farmer is one who has raised a bumper crop of good boys.

There's a new babyfood on the market. It's half orange juice and half garlic. It not only makes the baby healthier, but also easier to find in the dark.

Jelly is a food usually found on bread, children, and piano keys.

No family should have less than three children. If there is one genius among them, there should be two to support him.

Playing golf is like raising children — you keep thinking you'll do better next time.

It's real nice for children to have pets until the pets start having children.

Children are unpredictable. You never know when they're going to catch you in a lie.

Childhood is that wonderful period when all you need to do to lose weight is take a bath.

The children of today think they have it rough in school if they have to walk more than a block to park their cars.

Someday science may be able to explain why a child can't walk around a mud puddle.

Babies are angels whose wings grow shorter as their legs grow longer.

Children may tear up a house, but they never break up a home.

There's no child so bad that he can't be used as an income-tax deduction.

More twins are being born these days than ever before. Maybe kids lack the courage to come into the world alone.

A baby may not be able to lift very much, but it can hold a marriage together.

One reason so many children are seen on the streets at night is because they're afraid to stay home alone.

Children need strength to lean on, a shoulder to cry on, and an example to learn from.

You can get any child to run an errand for you — if you ask him at bedtime.

Maybe children could keep on the straight and narrow path if they could get information from someone who's been over the route.

Children are natural mimics; they act like their parents in spite of every effort to teach them good manners.

The best time to put the children to bed is when you can.

Nothing grieves a child more than to study the wrong lesson and learn something he wasn't supposed to.

The trouble with a child is that he can't grow up to be anything but an adult.

Children are about the only things in a modern home that have to be washed by hand.

Few children are guilty of thoughtless mischief. They plan it.

You can tell your kids are growing up when they stop asking where they came from and start refusing to say where they're going.

When a child listens to his mother, he's probably on the telephone extension.

Modern parents think children should be seen, not heard; children think parents should be neither seen nor heard.

Many children have grown up to be fairly levelheaded because their parents couldn't find the guidance book they were looking for.

What most children learn by doing is how to drive their parents almost crazy.

It's extremely difficult for a child to live right if he has never seen it done.

Children these days seem to grow up bigger and faster, yet remain children longer than ever before.

It's always charming to see little children lined up waiting to talk to the department store Santa Claus — some with parents, some with lists, and some with chicken pox.

Sending your child to college is like sending your clothes to the laundry. You get what you put in, but sometimes you can hardly recognize it.

The chief trouble with children is they are human.

It's great to have your children home from school. It takes your mind off your other troubles.

The best thing to spend on children is your time.

Telling children that school days are the happiest days of their lives doesn't give them much to look forward to.

There are no illegitimate children — only illegitimate parents.

Some books you can't put down, and others you dare not put down when there are children in the house.

A small boy is a pain in the neck when he's around and a pain in the heart when he's not.

Safety note for motorists: "Watch out for children — especially if they're driving cars."

Too often an abandoned child is one who is still living with his parents.

Children love to break things — especially rules.

Watch the kid who's cutting classes at school — he may be in training to be a congressman later in life.

Children are unpredictable. You never know how high up the wall they're going to drive you.

Children disgrace us in public by behaving just like we do at home.

It now costs more to amuse a child than it once did to educate his father.

The first thing a child learns when he gets a drum is that he's never going to get another one.

Today's kids call it "finding themselves." In the "good old days" it was called loafing.

Reasoning with children is what gives you something to do while discovering that you can't.

When children are seen and not heard it's apt to be through binoculars.

A child's ear is a delicate instrument that can't hear a parent's shout from the next room, but picks up the faintest tingle of the ice cream man's bell.

Children always brighten up a home. They never turn out the lights.

Children who are reared in homes of poverty have only two mealtime choices — take it or leave it.

The school kids in some towns are getting so tough that teachers are playing hooky.

Children are like wet cement. Whatever falls on them makes an impression.

An unusual child is one who asks his parents questions they can answer.

The latest class of underprivileged children are those whose parents own two cars — but no speedboat.

Almost every child would learn to write sooner if allowed to do homework on wet cement.

All some people need to make them happy is a change — and most of the time that's all a baby needs.

The best possible infant care is to keep one end full and the other end dry.

If you don't want your children to hear what you're saying, pretend you're talking to them.

If children didn't ask questions, they would never know what little adults know.

It's hard, if not impossible, to get a child to pay attention to you, especially when you're telling him something for his own good.

When a child pays attention to his parents, they're probably whispering.

There is just as much authority in the family today as there ever was — only now the children exercise it.

Nowadays children are called bright when they make remarks that used to call for a good spanking.

A modern son is one who finishes college and his dad at the same time.

There are three ways to get something done: do it yourself, hire someone to do it, or forbid your kids to do it.

Adolescence is when children start bringing up their parents.

Life's golden age is when the children are too old to need baby sitters and too young to borrow the family car.

An alarm clock is a device for awakening people who don't have small children.

The only thing that children wear out faster than shoes are parents and teachers.

A kid who learns the value of a dollar these days is certain to grow up cynical.

Small children start to school these days with a big advantage. They already know two letters of the alphabet — TV.

One thing most children save for a rainy day is lots of energy.

Children of today play a game called Zip Code. It's like Post Office but faster.

A child, like your stomach, doesn't need all you can afford to give it.

The reason some parents want their children to play the piano instead of the violin is that it's harder to lose a piano.

Children may be deductible, but they're still taxing.

There are only two things children will share willingly — communicable diseases and their mother's age.

If you are disgusted and upset with your children, just imagine how God must feel about His!

The trouble with having outspoken children is that you're frequently left holding the bag they let the cat out of.

Most kids can't understand why a country that makes atomic bombs would ban firecrackers.

Nothing seems to make children more affectionate than sticky hands.

Not all children sass their parents. Some don't pay that much attention.

Children will be children — even after they are fifty years old.

When parents can't or won't control their children in the home, it's extremely difficult for the government to control them on the streets.

If some children are as bright as their parents think they are, they should be looked at through sunglasses.

No two children are alike — particularly if one is yours and the other one isn't.

Some children are running everything around the house except errands.

Children are a comfort to us in our old age, and they help us to reach it a lot sooner.

One important way for us to help our children grow up is for us to grow up first.

July

Independence Day

In two hundred years we've gone from taxation with representation to taxation without relaxation.

Just because the Declaration of Independence says everyone is entitled to the pursuit of happiness, it doesn't mean the government should finance the chase.

More than two hundred years ago our forefathers declared that we should be able to tax ourselves. We have proved we could, and how!

Just about everybody will agree that our country is on the move, though there is plenty of argument about the direction.

This country needs closer agreement on what this country needs.

The fourth of July, 1776 — that's when we declared our freedom from unfair British taxation. Then, in 1777, we started our own system of unfair taxation.

It's extremely difficult to believe that America was founded to avoid excessive taxation.

The tree of liberty is one shrub that won't stand very much grafting.

Let's not fight for more liberty until we learn how to handle what we've got.

Personal liberty ends where public safety begins.

If ever a new Statue of Liberty is designed, it will quite likely be holding the bag instead of the torch.

No constitution, no court, no law can save liberty when it dies in the hearts and minds of men and women.

Liberty is not a gift of God but a hard-won achievement with the help of God.

Those who are rooting up the tree of liberty will certainly be crushed by its fall.

Liberty is dearly bought, continually paid for, and difficult to keep.

The cradle of liberty needs more vigilant baby sitters.

Every child comes into the world endowed with liberty, opportunity, and a share of the war debt.

If we are going to fight for the liberty to worship, we ought to make use of that liberty.

45

Liberty doesn't work as well in practice as it does in speeches.

There is no liberty worth anything which is not liberty under law.

Every human being has the liberty to do that which is good, just, and honest.

Liberty is the right to go just as far as the law allows.

What this country needs is not more liberty, but fewer people who take liberties with liberty.

The way to get ahead of Russia is to get behind America.

Americans are endowed with certain inalienable rights, but if we don't stick up for them somebody will come along and un-endow them.

A patriotic American likes to discuss the Constitution of the United States despite the fact he has never taken the time to read it.

A patriotic American never orders anything from a menu that he can't spell.

Many Americans love their country for the same reason a farmer loves his cow — because they can milk it.

Patriotism is the willingness to make any sacrifice as long as it won't hurt business.

Asking your boss for a raise is really a patriotic duty since the government needs that additional tax on your salary.

When patriotism becomes a dirty word, a nation is ready to be taken to the cleaners.

True patriotism is your conviction that this country is superior to all others because you were born in it!

Patriotism will probably never develop to the point of parading in honor of the "unknown taxpayer."

Anybody who thinks there's free speech everywhere in this country has never been on a psychiatrist's couch.

Sometimes free speech is greatly overpriced.

A wit in Nebraska says patriotism is that pain you feel in your neck when a foreigner wins a championship.

A man's country is not just a certain area of land. It is a principle, and patriotism is loyalty to that principle.

True patriotism should make the heart beat faster and the tongue wag slower.

A dyed-in-the-wool patriot is one who says he's sorry he has only one income to give to his country.

A patriot is the fellow who is always ready and willing to lay down your life for his country.

A patriot is a man working for his country's future instead of boasting of its past.

A well-informed American knows the lineup of baseball teams and about half the words of the "Star-Spangled Banner."

Two songs, "The Star-Spangled Banner" and "Melancholy Baby," need to be rewritten. The first, because very few can sing it; the second, because everybody can.

We need to change our National Anthem to "Deep in the Heart of Taxes."

People stand up when they hear our National Anthem — and fall down when they start to sing it.

A political platform is like the second stanza of our National Anthem. Everybody knows it's there, but very few know the words.

Freedom of speech is still guaranteed in Russia. You can say anything you want — at least once.

We're thankful we have free speech here in America — and equally thankful that there's no law requiring us to listen to it.

No nation is so poor that it cannot afford free speech.

The greatest danger to free speech is that many people who have it are too free with it.

Some women regard free speech, not as a right, but as a continuous obligation.

One of the great blessings about living in a democracy is that we have complete control over how we pay our taxes — cash, check, or money order.

A democracy is a country in which everybody has an equal right to feel superior to the other fellow.

Ours is a democracy where the rich and the poor are alike — both complain about taxes.

Democracy, like love, can survive almost any attack — except neglect and indifference.

The most important principle of democracy is that even a wrong guy has rights.

One of the disadvantages of a democracy is that the minority has the say and the majority has to pay.

A democracy is a system where a fellow who didn't vote can spend the rest of the year kicking about the candidate the other fellows elected.

The difference between communism and democracy is — plenty!

Democracy is a wonderful system. It permits you to vote for a politician, and then sit on the jury that tries him.

A democracy is a form of government that believes at least part of what you earn belongs to you.

While living in a democracy, you can say what you think without thinking.

Democracy is a word all politicians use, and very few seem to understand.

Too many people see democracy as a chance to push other people around for their own personal benefit.

The United States would be better off if we had less conversation and more conservation.

What's wrong with our country isn't the people trying to get something for nothing — it's those who are succeeding.

The United States is a country of quiet majorities and vociferous minorities.

Relax, the United States will never run out of things to run out of.

U. S. now stands for Unlimited Spending.

What a great country this is! Anybody can have a second house, a second car, a second TV. All it takes is a second job, a second mortgage, and a second wind.

About all the United States is getting to see of the dove of peace is the bill.

A great man has said that the United States is having a rendezvous with destiny, but at times it seems more like it is having a blind date with fate.

The United States is a land with a President for a head, a Supreme Court for a backbone, and Congress for lungs.

The United States is determined that there shall be no more wars and is equally determined to be ready for the next one.

We ought to be thankful that we are living in a country where folks can say what they think without thinking.

A democracy is a place where you can say what you please but don't have to listen unless you want to.

Democracy cannot be safe anywhere until it is safe everywhere.

A democracy is government that is run by all the people and run down by some of them.

Democracy would not need so many to defend it if it had more on whom it could depend.

Freedom is not the right to do as you please, but the liberty to do as you ought.

If all men are born free, why doesn't somebody tell the hospitals and doctors about it?

Freedom is like the air we breathe; we don't miss it until we're deprived of it.

Freedom ends when it begins to deprive another of his freedom.

This country is as free today as it ever was — unless you happen to be a taxpayer.

Freedom is the right all people have to be as happy as they can.

Freedom is indivisible. It is for all or none.

We live in a wonderful country where lawns are well-kept — and laws aren't!

Religious freedom is the right of each individual to attend the church of his choice, or go fishing.

Freedom is the sure possession of only those who have the courage to defend it.

Freedom is a jealous mistress. To possess her, we must reject her ancient competitor, slavery. She will not accept a divided allegiance.

If freedom is important when we don't have it, why shouldn't it be just as important when we do have it?

Freedom departs when we are no longer worthy of possessing it.

Our freedoms are lost unless they are continually fought for.

One of the best freedoms is the freedom from bad habits.

No freedom is so outrageously and so often abused as the freedom of speech.

Future generations will be born free, equal, and in debt.

As a general rule, the freedom of any people can be judged by the volume of their laughter.

The tree of liberty is one shrub that won't stand very much grafting.

No man should govern another man without the other's consent.

Newspapers are owned by individuals and corporations, but freedom of the press belongs to the people.

We should be extremely happy living in a country where we put chains on tires and not on people.

In 1776 our country was unsettled — it still is!

The principal export of the United States is money.

Many a man who is proud of his right to say what he pleases wishes he had the courage to do so.

Usually the man who howls loudest about free speech has nothing worth saying.

No freedom is so outrageously and so often abused as the freedom of speech.

It's fortunate that we have freedom of speech, but it's unfortunate that the supply usually exceeds the demand.

In this country you are still privileged to free speech, but that's as far as the Constitution goes. It doesn't guarantee listeners.

Freedom not to listen is just as precious as freedom of speech.

Too many people confuse free speech with loose talk.

Why shouldn't speech be free? Very little of it is worth anything.

The only place in America where you don't have free speech is in a telephone booth.

Freedom of speech is useless unless you have something to say.

Freedom of speech is the right to argue about issues you don't understand.

Some wit has said that freedom of speech means that even a donkey has a right to bray!

The fact that you know what to say does not guarantee your right or obligation to say it.

An election year is when a lot of politicians get free speech mixed up with cheap talk.

A long-winded speaker should realize that, while the Constitution guarantees free speech, it doesn't guarantee listeners.

Ambition in America is still rewarded — with high taxes.

Never in the history of America have so few loused up so much for so many.

America is always a land of promise in an election year.

One reason America is great is because we have been unable to exhaust our natural resources in spite of our best efforts.

The donkey and the elephant play important roles in American politics. The bull plays a major role too.

America is a country where permanent waves are increasing and permanent wives are decreasing.

In America we'll try anything once — except criminals.

Our forefathers founded an enduring republic that has had to endure a lot more than they thought it would have to endure.

America may be the land of the free, but not the debt-free.

One quarter of America is covered with forests and the rest with beer cans.

America has drive-in theaters, drive-in supermarkets, drive-in restaurants, and drive-in banks. What it needs now are more drive-in parking places.

Foreign observers say America is no longer a young country — it's fast reaching meddle age.

America is a land of six-lane highways, one-way streets, and four-way cold tablets.

The beauty of America is that the average man always thinks he's above average.

America has the highest standard of living in the world. Now let's raise our standard of thinking.

Naturalists who claim America's wildlife is disappearing don't stay up very late at night.

America is the only country in the world where it takes more brains to make out the income tax return than it does to make the income.

There are two things in America that are growing bigger together — garbage cans and taxes.

America is a land where, thanks to its high birthrate, people are being born faster than the automobile can kill them.

According to recent reports, America produces 92 percent of the world's natural gas — not counting the speeches of our senators and congressmen.

America is rapidly achieving a high standard of poverty.

The way to get ahead of Russia is to get behind America.

What is hurting America today is the high cost of low living.

America is a country where Groucho Marx has more followers than Karl Marx.

Much has been said about what America stands for. Let's not forget some things that America won't stand for.

You can say what you please in America — but nobody listens.

America has some fine old ruins. Many of them can be seen in our nightclubs.

Maybe this country would not be in such a mess today if the Indians had adopted more stringent immigration laws.

It's hard to believe that America was founded to avoid high taxation.

America's number one energy crisis is Monday morning.

The trouble with America today is that all the stupid people are cocksure of everything and all the intelligent people are full of doubt.

America unquestionably has the highest standard of living in the world. Too bad we can't afford it.

One thing America isn't running out of is debts.

Freedom also includes the right to mismanage your own affairs.

America is rapidly proving to be a place with two cars in every garage — and none of them paid for.

America was better off when folks opened meals with a prayer instead of a can opener.

America has more transportation facilities than any other nation, but they're so crowded we can't use them.

Our country was in better condition when there were more whittlers and fewer chiselers.

America has turned out some great men, but there are others not so great that ought to be turned out.

America is the land of the spree and the home of the crave.

Americans are a religious people. You can tell they trust in God by the way they drive.

There are too many middle-of-the-roaders in America, and they all drive cars.

Our forefathers built this country with three tools: an ax, a plow, and a book. That book was the Bible.

Our beloved country recently celebrated its two-hundredth birthday, and all we've learned in that time is how to go fast, work less, waste more, and die quicker.

It's easy to believe that any American boy can become president when you observe some of them who have.

Most kids can't understand why a country that makes atomic bombs would ban firecrackers.

In some foreign countries girls dress like their mothers, but in America it's the other way around.

In America it's "Believe it or not," but in communist countries it's "Believe it or else."

It is impossible to mentally and socially enslave a Bible-reading people.

America leads the world in the highway distribution of beer cans.

What America really needs most are those things which money can't buy.

America is a land of opportunity. Everybody can become a taxpayer.

As the IRS sees it, America is a land of untold wealth.

If you think free speech costs you nothing, try listening to some of it.

Creating all men free and equal isn't enough. Some means must be devised to keep them free and equal.

Freedom is not only the right to use your judgment, but the obligation to live with the consequences.

Freedom is not worth having if it does not include the freedom to make mistakes.

When freedom grows flabby, the tyrants become grabby.

The freedom of the press these days is the freedom to be sure that all the propaganda is on one side.

We have an abundance of freedom in this country, even the freedom to make fools of ourselves.

We may rest assured that freedom is worth whatever it costs.

Freedom is a package deal — with it comes responsibilities and consequences.

Men fight for freedom and then start making laws to get rid of it.

Too many people are clamoring for freedom to do what ought not to be done.

The freedom of slaves is measured by the length of their chains.

Whether or not this is a free country depends on what you want to do.

Under the Constitution of the United States every man has the right to make a fool of himself as he sees fit.

Communism will be defeated in America and in all countries where Christians are more interested in being mobilized than in being tranquilized.

Americans have always been willing to pay any price for freedom. If you don't believe it, look at the divorce statistics!

Freedom, like soap, can lose its strength if watered down.

In America today there is a surplus of food, a surplus of manufactured goods, and a surplus of people who think they know how to run the government.

A Communist in the United States is a person who says everything is perfect in Russia but stays in this country because he likes to rough it.

Why did they have to admit to the Union the State of Confusion?

Anybody who thinks conversation is a lost art in America doesn't play bridge.

It's now costing Americans twice as much to live beyond their means as it did twenty years ago.

Foreign aggressors don't realize that even if they invaded the United States they couldn't afford to live here.

The crime situation is so bad in some American cities you could walk five blocks and never leave the scene of the crime.

The United States is running out of things our grandfathers never imagined anybody would need.

Diplomats are frequently decorated in European countries. We'd like to crown some of ours here in this country.

The American dream is owning a British sports car, smoking a Havana cigar, and drinking Russian vodka on the French Riviera.

The way the American economy is going, we'll soon have a system of checks and bounces.

What this country needs today is fewer experts on what this country needs.

Not as many people have lost faith in America as you might think. An awful lot of them still sign up for a thirty-year mortgage.

The trouble with some American families is that they have Cadillac tastes and compact incomes.

It often seems like the United States is building up its enemies and flattening its taxpayers.

This country is as free today as it ever was — unless you happen to be a taxpayer.

In this country you are still privileged to free speech, but that's as far as the Constitution goes. It doesn't guarantee listeners.

Don't you long for the "good old days" when Uncle Sam lived within his income and without most of yours?

The American family and the United States government are in agreement about one thing — neither of them can live within their income.

Income-tax forms should be more realistic by allowing the taxpayer to list Uncle Sam as a dependent.

Americans will pay a big price for an invention that will help them save time they don't know what to do with.

The people of the United States don't need more judges, but more sound judgment.

Everybody says the country has too many laws, and yet every man thinks he knows of a law that ought to be passed.

In Russia the people have only what the government gives them; in America the people have only what the government does not take away from them in taxes.

The thing raised most abundantly in the United States is taxes.

The United States is still the land of opportunity. Where else could you earn enough money to pay the interest on what you owe?

The young people of the United States squander over ten billion dollars a year on games of chance. This does not include weddings, starting a business, passing cars on a hill, or buying a television set.

In Africa certain of the native tribes practice the strange custom of beating the ground with clubs and uttering wild bloodcurdling yells. Anthropologists call this a form of primitive expression. In America we call it golf.

Nothing in recent years seems to have improved the health of the American people as much as the staggering cost of being sick.

There are three stages in American history: the passing of the buffalo, the passing of the Indian, and the passing of the buck.

In many ways the past two hundred years of our history have changed this country from independence to government dependence.

Which has made the biggest liars out of Americans — golf or the income tax?

The following is the revised edition of an American prayer: "Forgive us our debts, O Lord, as we forgive our international debtors."

If only men took the nation's problems as seriously as they do its sports!

The main difference between Russia and the United States is that in Russia the state owns everything and in the United States the finance companies do.

The president has the next to the hardest job in the United States. The taxpayer has the hardest.

The United States is in worse condition than we might think. Every time we dial a prayer we get a busy signal.

Anybody who thinks the United States isn't still the land of promise just hasn't been listening to political speeches lately.

September

Labor Day

The plain fact is that human beings are happy only when they are striving for something worthwhile.

A great deal of poor health in this country may be attributed to heavy meals and light work.

Sign at highway construction site: "Men working — we hope."

The ideal of some men is to marry a rich girl who is too proud to have her husband work.

Some fellows dream of worthy accomplishments, while others stay awake and do them.

If you want a place in the sun, you will have to expect some blisters.

Just over the hill is a beautiful valley, but you must climb the hill to see it.

God gives us the ingredients for our daily bread, but He expects us to do the baking.

Our ship would come in much sooner if we'd only swim out to meet it.

You can often gauge a man's ambition by whether he hates his alarm clock or considers it his dear friend.

Opportunity has the uncanny habit of favoring those who have paid the price of years of preparation.

Nothing worthwhile is achieved without patience, labor, and disappointment.

The man of the hour spent many days and nights getting there.

Most of us would be in more trouble than we are if all our prayers had been answered.

Ambition never gets anywhere until it forms a partnership with work.

Watch out for ambition! It can get you into a lot of hard work.

America's number one energy crisis is Monday morning.

If you want to go far in business, you'll have to stay close to it.

You can tell a man's character by what he turns up when offered a job — his nose or his sleeves.

Christianity, like a watch, needs to be wound regularly if it is to be kept running.

Many people think life would be so much more enjoyable if we didn't have to work our way through it.

Life is like a poker game — if you don't put anything in the pot, there won't be anything to take out.

We get out of life what we put into it — that's the trouble!

To love and to labor is the sum of life; and, yet, how many think they are living when they neither love nor labor?

A task worth doing and friends worth having make life worthwhile.

Luck is a wonderful thing. The harder a person works, the more of it he seems to have.

Good luck is a lazy man's estimate of a worker's success.

Good luck often has the odor of perspiration about it.

It's hard to recognize good luck. It looks so much like something you've earned!

The best medicine in the world is to love your work and your enemies.

There are a lot of men in this world who started at the bottom — and stayed there.

Most men can't tell the difference between working up steam and generating fog.

Nervous prostration was unknown when people worked more and worried less.

You can qualify as an old-timer if you can remember when people didn't need any more than a day to do a day's work.

The reason a lot of people can't find opportunity is that it is often disguised as hard work.

Even when opportunity knocks, a man still has to get off his seat and open the door.

It will be a great day when everybody who has a job is working.

Hard work rarely kills because so few give it a chance.

Most of us pray for more things than we are willing to work for.

One blessing in being poor, honest, and hard-working is that nobody envies you.

Heads, hearts, and hands could settle the world's problems better than arms.

Religion is like a wheelbarrow — you have to push it.

What's all this talk about getting rich the hard way? Is there any other way?

The trouble with the road to riches these days is there are too many toll booths along the way.

Selling is quite easy if you work hard enough at it.

A successful man continues to look for work after he has found a job.

Behind every successful man there are usually a lot of unsuccessful years.

Many people carefully avoid discovering the secret of success because deep down they suspect the secret may be hard work.

You don't have to lie awake nights to succeed; just stay awake days.

All men want to succeed, but some men want to succeed so much they're willing to work to achieve it.

The dictionary is the only place where success comes before work.

Success is sweet, but its secret is sweat.

No one has yet climbed the ladder of success with his hands in his pockets.

Most people do only what they are required to do, but successful people do a little more.

You won't find many rules for success that will work unless you do.

One of the hardest ways to make a living is to work for it.

Almost any system will work if the people behind it will.

Lots of people don't have to look at the world through rose-colored glasses — their eyes are already bloodshot.

No dream comes true until you wake up and go to work.

A drunkard can't make both ends meet because he's too busy making one end drink.

Economists predict the year ahead will reward hard workers. What a frightening outlook for many!

We won't go far without enthusiasm, but neither will we go far if that's all we have.

Enthusiasm for hard work is most sincerely expressed by the person who is paying for it.

Don't envy anybody. Every person has something no other person has. Develop that one thing and make it outstanding.

An executive is one who hires others to do the work he's supposed to do.

Often an expert is the fellow you employ to do what you'd rather not.

Families that pray together stay together, and families that work together — eat.

The farmer doesn't go to work. He wakes up every morning surrounded by it.

The American farmer prefers getting bent from hard work rather than getting crooked from trying to avoid it.

Mankind's worst enemy is fear — of work!

Most modern girls detest four-letter words such as wash, iron, cook, and dust.

The modern girl's hair may look like a mop, but that doesn't seem to worry her — she doesn't know what a mop looks like.

For some girls the idea of housework is to sweep the floor with a glance.

God created the world in six days — which probably never could have happened if there had been labor unions.

Happiness is the result of being too busy to be miserable.

A man has happiness in the palm of his hands if he can fill his days with real work and his nights with real rest.

The happiest people are those who are too busy to notice whether they are happy or not.

What the church needs is more men who talk less and work more.

What the church needs today is more calloused hands and fewer calloused hearts.

It seems that our modern churches are full of willing people; some are willing to work, and others are willing to let them.

There are two periods when Congress does no business: one is before the holidays; and the other, after.

The dentist is one guy who's always ready to get back to the old grind.

If you burn the candle at both ends you are not as bright as you think.

The best kind of pride is that which compels a man to do his best work — even when no one is looking.

If we take care of our work, the results of our work will take care of us.

Hard work won't kill a fellow if he can stay far enough away from it.

There's a difference between working every day and having a perfect attendance record.

The more steam you put behind your work, the louder you can whistle when it's done.

Dodging work is the hardest work of all and yields the poorest returns.

The best way to criticize the other fellow's work is to do yours better.

Most people like work. It fascinates them. They can sit and look at it for hours.

The only state that permits a woman to work more than eight hours a day is the state of matrimony.

It may be that hard work is respectable, but that doesn't make it popular.

Do what you are told to do and then some. It's the "then some" that gets your salary raised.

If hard work is the key to success, most people would rather pick the lock.

Faith may move mountains, but only hard work can put a tunnel through.

The thing that makes it so tough to find fault with some people's work is that they never do any.

Hard work never hurt anybody who happened to be wealthy enough to hire somebody else to do it.

Work is the annoyance people have to endure between coffee breaks.

How long a woman works after her marriage is often determined by the number of payments still due on her husband's car.

Many years ago they didn't put up signs reading, "Men Working," but back then you could tell what they were doing.

It is especially hard to work for money you've already spent for something you didn't need.

With so many parking difficulties, household errands, and golf, it's almost impossible for a man to find any time for his work.

Hard work never killed anybody, but some of us sure don't want to take the chance of being the first victim.

Sign in a supermarket in Springfield, Illinois: "Wanted — clerk to work eight hours a day to replace one who didn't."

Work, of course, is the cure for unrest, but there are lots of people who think the remedy is worse than the disease.

July is the time of year when the fellow who worked so hard to graduate wonders what the hurry was.

If you think you work harder than the average worker, you're an average worker.

The reason why so many men can't work any harder in the office is because they wear leisure suits.

A lot of people are already working a four day week, though it takes them five or six days to do it.

Committee work is like a soft chair — easy to get into but hard to get out of.

Hard work is usually an accumulation of easy things that should have been done last week.

Just about the time a woman's work is done for the day, her husband asks her to help him with the dishes.

Hard work never hurts people who don't do any.

The world's work must be done by some of us. We can't all be politicians and efficiency experts.

Most people like hard work. This is particularly true when they're paying for it.

Organized labor is all right until it becomes organized loafing.

A few people are enthusiastic about work, but most of the time they're the bosses.

The Lord didn't burden us with work. He blessed us with it.

Working hard means going all out until you're all in.

The only thing you can get without work is debt.

When you see some people work you wonder what they'll do when they retire.

The hardest work some people do is describing the work they do.

The trouble with a lot of folks these days is they want to have their work cut out for them — completely!

The young man who is able to work his way through college is a pretty good bet to be able to work his way through life.

The man who doesn't do more than he's paid for isn't worth what he gets.

Father must work for two reasons: Christmas and vacation.

One thing that keeps a lot of people from being a success is work.

If you want to succeed, wear out two pairs of shoes to every suit.

Industry is the mother of success — luck, a distant relative.

Success is the result of backbone, not wishbone.

If you gave the same amount of time to your work as you do your church, how long would you hold your job?

The minimum wage has gone up considerably. Wouldn't it be wonderful if we could just do something about the minimum effort?

The hardest work in the world is that which should have been done yesterday.

A woman's work is never done, especially if she asks her husband to do it.

People who do a good day's work won't have much competition.

Hard work and devotion to duty will surely get you a promotion — unless, of course, the boss has a relative who wants the job.

We can't remember seeing a man get bent over from hard work, but we've seen a lot of them go broke without it.

If you think hard work never hurt anybody, you've never paid for any.

Keeping on top of your work is better than letting your work get on top of you.

Work is the best thing ever invented for killing time.

Worry kills more people than work. Some people play it safe by doing neither.

Nothing is hard work unless there's something else you'd rather do.

All things come to him who goes after what the other fellow waits for.

Speaking of tranquilizers, even back in grandpa's day there was something to make a fellow sleep — they called it work.

Work is one of the greatest things in the world. So don't you think we should save some of it for tomorrow?

Unless we all work for the common good there won't be any.

Everybody has to work for the government — but only the bureaucrats get paid for it.

If you do all the work and somebody else gets the credit — he's probably your boss.

It is better to become bent from hard work than to become crooked without it.

It's predicted that in twenty years people will work two days a week and relax five. Some employers think that's happening now.

The thing most of us don't like about work is that it's so daily.

Folks keep saying that hard work never killed anybody. Come to think of it, we never heard of anybody resting themselves to death either.

The trouble with getting to work on time is that it makes the day so long.

A man should work eight hours and sleep eight hours, but not the same eight hours.

Nowadays when you miss a day's work the government loses as much as you do.

About the only folks who work like a horse these days have a boss riding them.

One way to boost production in this country would be to put the labor bosses to work.

A man's work is a portrait of himself.

Many people are willing to do any kind of work which does not require standing, sitting, bending, or lying down.

It's extremely difficult for men of different nations to work together when they carry a rifle on one shoulder and a chip on the other.

Human beings, like chickens, thrive best when they have to scratch for what they get.

Some people are too heavy for light work, and others are too light for heavy work.

About the only way work can kill a fellow is to scare him to death.

Work isn't work if you like it.

Never buy anything with a handle on it. It might mean work!

Hard work is the yeast that raises the dough.

Two things deprive people of their peace of mind: work unfinished, and work not yet begun.

Many people don't mind going to work — it's the long wait until quitting time that irritates them.

Fortunately, in our work there is always a choice. We can do it willingly or unwillingly.

The advantage of working day and night is that you can probably earn enough to pay the doctor when you have a nervous breakdown.

Work is a tonic that contains no habit-forming drugs.

Men who dream of hitching their wagon to a star would be better off to hitch up their pants and go to work.

The reason worry kills more people than work is that people worry more than they work.

Grandpa and grandma were too busy scratching for a living to need books on how to stop worrying.

Two good openings for a young man are the legs in a pair of overalls.

Work hard. The job you save may be your own.

Some will give an honest day's work even if it takes them all week to do it.

There seems to be no cure for those who are allergic to work.

It's simply fantastic the amount of work you can get done if you don't do anything else.

Housework is something you do that nobody notices unless you don't do it.

Some people are so superstitious they won't work any week that has a Friday in it.

Grandparents' Day

A man begins to show his age at about the same time he begins to show pictures of his grandchildren.

Nothing makes a boy smarter than being a grandson.

More children are spoiled because the parents won't spank Grandma.

Just about the time a woman thinks her work is done, she becomes a grandmother.

Grandparents are people who come to your house, spoil the children, and then go home.

No cowboy was ever faster on the draw than a grandparent pulling a baby picture out of a wallet.

Another thing "so simple a child can operate" is a grandparent.

Our grandparents never dreamed that the steering wheel would become America's only family circle.

A grandmother is a baby sitter who watches the kids instead of the television.

Grandchildren don't make a man feel old — it's knowing that he's married to a grandmother.

Grandpa and grandma were too busy scratching for a living to need books on how to stop worrying.

Nothing is harder on a grandparent than having to watch a grandchild being disciplined.

Some of our modern grandmothers are so young and spry they help the Boy Scouts across the street.

Sign on an antique shop in Stockton, California: "Come in and buy what your grandmother threw away."

October

Mother-in-Law's Day

The penalty for bigamy is two mothers-in-law.

The wife isn't always boss in the American home. Sometimes it's her mother.

The most terrible thing about a divorce is that somewhere, maybe miles apart, two mothers are nodding their heads and saying, "See? I told you so."

To the average husband, the "blessed event" is when his mother-in-law goes home.

English law prohibits a man from marrying his mother-in-law. This is the epitome of useless legislation.

"Double trouble" is a mother-in-law with a twin sister.

Listen men: Maybe you'll never be as big a hero as your son thinks you are but you'll never be as big a fool as your mother-in-law thinks your are either!

The young mother gets along beautifully with her mother-in-law because she probably can't afford a baby sitter.

No man is really successful until his mother-in-law admits it.

A man is seldom as smart as his mother thinks, or as dumb as his mother-in-law says he is.

When it comes to broken marriages most husbands will split the blame — half his wife's fault, and half her mother's.

Boss's Day

When they say a man is a "born executive," they mean his father owns the business.

A good executive is one who can make decisions quickly — and sometimes correctly.

Plaque on the desk of an executive: "Once I thought I was wrong — but I was mistaken."

Some executives call passing the buck delegating authority.

A certain ineffective executive was recently fired. No one filled his vacancy. He didn't leave one.

Authority is like a bank account. The more you draw on it, the less you have.

Some men who speak with authority at work know enough to bow to a higher authority at home.

Executive ability is the art of getting credit for all the hard work that somebody else does.

An executive is a fellow who can take as long as he wants to make a snap decision.

One of the greatest failings of our present-day executive is his inability to do what he's supposed to do.

A survey shows that slender executives make more money than fat ones. The chunky son of the president is apt to be an exception.

Sign on a junior executive's desk: "It's not whether you win or lose — it's how you place the blame.

An executive refused an employee's request for a raise, adding, "I know you can't get married on what I pay you —and some day you'll thank me."

An executive reports that his secretary is making two hundred a week. Not dollars — mistakes!

Some big executives have computers to do all their thinking for them. Some just have wives.

The executive most hated by those around him is the one who is always annoying office workers by asking them to do something.

A business executive in Denver gave his employees long vacations to find out which ones he could do without.

An executive is one who hires others to do the work he's supposed to do.

The best executive is the one who has sense enough to pick good people to do what he wants done, and self-restraint enough to keep from meddling with them while they do it.

An executive is a man who talks to the visitors while others are doing the work.

The chief executive of a large business firm in Milwaukee told his underlings at an office meeting, "The day of the yes-man is over. Does everybody agree?"

With some executives the real test of a good idea is whether they thought of it first.

Executives of large industrial firms are looking for men between twenty-five and thirty with forty years of experience.

Sign on an executive's desk: "Don't tell me what I mean. Let me figure it out myself."

If you want a job done fast, give it to a busy executive. He'll have his secretary do it.

A good executive is judged by the company he keeps — solvent.

Slogan of a new executive: "If you haven't developed ulcers, you're not carrying your share of the load."

An honest executive is one who shares the credit with the man who did all the work.

A modern executive is a man who wears out his clothes at the seat of his pants first.

Sign on a Chicago executive's desk: "It's too late to agree with me. I've already changed my mind."

An overbearing boss seldom fires you — he just makes you wish he had.

Some bosses are so mean that if they pay you a compliment they expect to get a receipt.

The wife isn't always boss in the American home. Sometimes it's her mother.

If your boss doesn't pay you what you deserve, be thankful!

Some bosses take great pains — and give them to others.

Be loyal to your boss because the next one might be worse.

The worst boss anyone can have is a bad habit.

You may know more than your employer, but his knowledge pays off.

The man who laughs at his boss's jokes doesn't necessarily have a sense of humor, but he surely has a sense of direction.

It is generally understood that leisure time is what you have when the boss is on vacation.

The best time to start thinking about retirement is before your boss does.

He who laughs last at the boss's jokes probably isn't very far from retirement.

Ulcers are contagious. You can get them from your boss.

Vacations are easy to plan — the boss tells you when, and the wife tells you where.

The reason a great many men don't bring their boss home for dinner is because she is already there.

If you do all the work and somebody else gets the credit — he's probably your boss.

A few people are enthusiastic about work, but most of the time they're the bosses.

About the only folks who work like a horse these days have a boss riding them.

One way to boost production in this country would be to put the labor bosses to work.

Hard work and devotion to duty will surely get you a promotion — unless, of course, the boss has a relative who wants the job.

Ability is what will get you to the top if the boss has no daughter.

Before you have an argument with your boss, you'd better take a good look at both sides — his side and the outside.

Before arguing with your boss, make absolutely sure you're right — then let the matter drop.

The only time it's safe to tell the boss where to get off is when he falls asleep on the bus.

Watch the man who says he's the boss at home. He may lie about other things too.

The hardest job in the world is telling the boss the computer proved him wrong.

A certain boss when asked how many people work for him replied, "About half of them."

Pity the boss. He has to come in early to see who comes in late.

In any office you can tell who the boss is: he's the one watching the clock during the coffee break.

Nothing makes a man the boss of his house like living alone.

Computers will never replace man entirely until they learn to laugh at the boss's jokes.

A man's best boss is a well-trained conscience.

Being diplomatic is telling your boss he has an open mind instead of telling him he has a hole in the head.

Nothing is quite as embarrassing as watching your boss do something you assured him couldn't be done.

The fellow who is fired with enthusiasm for his work is seldom fired by his boss.

Enthusiasm for hard work is most sincerely expressed by the person who is paying for it.

The fellow who can beat his boss at golf is usually prudent enough not to.

The man is still boss in the American home — as long as he allows his wife to make all the decisions.

A husband often thinks he bosses the house — but actually he only houses the boss.

A husband wanted to show his wife who was boss so he bought her a mirror.

Imagination is what makes the average man think he can run the business better than his boss.

Nothing improves a joke more than telling it to your employees.

The fellow who knows more than his boss should be careful to conceal it.

November

Election Day

A democracy is a system where a fellow who didn't vote can spend the rest of the year kicking about the candidate the other fellows elected.

The cheapest way to have your family tree traced is to run for public office.

People are not against political jokes — they just wonder how they get elected.

Everybody makes mistakes. That's why we keep having political elections.

Ballot boxes in America are more often starved than stuffed.

Be thankful American elections are by ballots — not bullets. We count the returns — not the remains.

It's nice to have four years between elections. It takes people that long to regain their faith.

During political elections all political parties campaign for better education. When we take a close look at some of the men elected, we have to admit it's needed.

It is reported that someone recently broke into the Kremlin and stole next year's election.

Russia is just about the only country in the world where nobody sits up all night to see how the elections come out.

Russia is a gambler's paradise; you'd never lose an election bet.

If we could use the money political candidates spend on their campaigns, we could cure a lot of the ills they complain about.

We are sorely in need of a voting machine with a space for "Remarks."

It's useless to try to hold some people to anything they say while they're madly in love, drunk, or running for office.

You can't fool all the people all the time, but politicans figure that once every four years is good enough.

Everytime a politician expresses a growing concern for something the price goes up.

The election isn't very far away when a candidate can recognize you across the street.

Wasn't it too bad about the politician in Ohio who ran for reelection unopposed — and lost?

An election year is when a lot of politicians get free speech mixed up with cheap talk.

We are all ready to vote a straight ticket next election — as soon as we can find out which party is straight.

It's about time that voters start electing candidates for what they won't stand for.

Don't vote a straight ticket unless it's filled with straight men.

An election year is a period when all the Democrats and all the Republicans devote their time saving the country from each other.

During an election year the political races get rough, and many candidates develop straddle sores.

The guy who never votes is the first to tell you what's wrong with the government.

The whole purpose of any political campaign is to stay calm, cool, and elected.

In this country only half of the voters vote and generally it's the wrong half.

An election is a system which allows us to decide which politicians we prefer to mess things up for us.

The most dangerous vote in America is the vote that is not used.

We should hold elections every year because there never seem to be tax increases in an election year.

Veteran's Day

History has seen wars which used up less ammunition than a cease-fire does today.

The best place to hold productive peace conferences is a few hundred yards behind the lines of battle.

Peace is a period of confusion and unrest between two wars.

Perpetual peace seems as far removed as perpetual motion.

Peace won by the compromise of principles is a short-lived achievement.

The world will never be the dwelling place of peace until peace has found a home in the heart of each and every man.

Every war causes soldiers to change nearly all their ideas, except their opinion of officers.

The key to lasting peace is to rely less on arms and more on heads.

What the nations of the world need is a peace conference with the "Prince of Peace."

A military inductee, when asked if he had any physical defects, replied, "No guts."

Wars are never caused by the little men, just fought by them.

There will be no peace as long as God remains unseated at the conference table.

Thanksgiving

The greatest lesson we learn from past civilizations is ingratitude.

If you can't be content with what you have received, be thankful for what you have escaped.

A man gave a woman his seat on the bus; she fainted. When she revived, she thanked him; then he fainted.

There's one thing for which you should be thankful — only you and God have all the facts about yourself.

Our favorite attitude should be gratitude.

He who is not grateful for the good things he has would not be happy with what he wishes he had.

Debts of gratitude are the most difficult to collect.

Gratitude to God should be as regular as our heartbeat.

He who forgets the language of gratitude can never be on speaking terms with happiness.

There is a sense in which no gift is ours till we have thanked the giver.

Gratitude is the rarest of all virtues, and yet we invariably expect it.

He who receives a good turn should never forget it; he who does one should never remember it.

The worst possible moment for an atheist is when he feels grateful and has no one to thank.

Be grateful for what you have, not regretful for what you haven't.

If you can't be grateful for what you receive, be grateful for what you escape.

Gratitude is not only the greatest of virtues, but the parent of all the others.

Be grateful for the doors of opportunity — and for friends who oil the hinges.

If you have nothing to be thankful for, make up your mind that there is something wrong with you.

There's always something to be thankful for. If you can't pay your bills, you can be thankful you're not one of your creditors.

If you have nothing for which to be thankful, make up your mind that there's something wrong with you.

Be thankful if your job is a little harder than you like. A razor can't be sharpened on a piece of velvet.

We should be thankful for the good things that we have and, also, for the bad things we don't have.

A person doesn't realize how much he has to be thankful for until he has to pay taxes on it.

Even though we can't have all we want, we ought to be thankful we don't get what we deserve.

We ought to be thankful that we are living in a country where folks can say what they think without thinking.

There's one thing for which you should be abundantly thankful — only you and God have all the facts about yourself.

Thankfulness could well be the finest sentiment of man — and also the rarest.

It isn't what you have in your pocket that makes you thankful, but what you have in your heart.

Gratitude is the most exquisite form of courtesy.

Happiness comes when we stop wailing about the troubles we have, and offer thanks for all the troubles we don't have.

Our next Thanksgiving menu will probably consist of roast turkey, yams, and pickled relatives.

If you think you haven't much to be thankful for, why not be thankful for some of the things you *don't* have?

Let us give thanks — if only for all the bad things that are never going to happen.

December

Christmas

Let's all have an old-fashioned Christmas this year, but not the kind that comes in bottles.

Many a parent sighs for the "good old days" when a stocking could hold what a child wanted for Christmas.

The Christmas season reminds us that a demonstration of religion is often better than a definition of it.

Christmas shoppers are people with the "brotherly shove."

Smart kids will be hanging up stretch stockings next Christmas.

Christmas is the time of year when both trees and husbands get trimmed. Sometimes both get lit up too.

You might as well do your Christmas hinting early.

Christmas is a time for sportsmanship because we don't always get everything we want.

We feel close to everybody at Christmas — especially on a bus.

What many a store clerk gets for Christmas is an ulcer.

The Christmas spirit that goes out with the dried-up Christmas tree is just as worthless.

There have always been some Christmas stockings that provided Santa with a few problems, but one wonders about his reaction to panty hose!

The exchange of Christmas gifts ought to be reciprocal rather than retaliatory.

Keeping Christmas is good, but sharing it with others is much better.

The best Christmas gift of all is the presence of a happy family all wrapped up with one another.

Christmas is a time when a lot of others besides Santa find themselves in the red.

At Christmas most parents spend more money on their children than they did on the honeymoon that started it all.

A father's biggest difficulty at Christmas time is convincing the children that he is Santa Claus and his wife that he is not.

Christmas is a race to see which gives out first — your money or your feet.

The Christmas season is only as meaningful as we make it.

Christmas carolers sing about peace on earth, but they don't tell us where.

Can you remember when Christmas was so simple that one Santa Claus could work an entire town?

What most of us want for Christmas is the day after.

Anyone who thinks Christmas doesn't last all year doesn't have a charge account.

About all you can do is dream of a white Christmas, for it seems like it always leaves most of us in the red.

The average couple splits the Christmas chores. She signs the cards and he signs the checks.

Christmas shopping should include buying toys for the children that their father would enjoy playing with.

Last year a big store in Milwaukee started its Christmas sale so early that Santa Claus wore Bermuda shorts.

Christmas is a time when everybody wants his past forgotten and his present remembered.

Always mail your Christmas gift early. It will give the receiver time to reciprocate.

Christmas is the time of the year when Santa Claus comes down the chimney and your savings go down the drain.

When we throw out the Christmas tree we should be especially careful not to throw out the Christmas spirit with it.

Christmas holidays mean: anticipation, preparation, recreation, prostration, and recuperation.

A Christmas shopper's complaint is one of long-standing.

Christmas is when we celebrate the birth of the Prince of Peace by giving our kids rockets, machine guns, atom-bomb kits, and tanks.

Perhaps the best Yuletide decoration is being wreathed in smiles.

An unbreakable Christmas toy is one that's guaranteed to last through the New Year.

This year Americans are planning the biggest Christmas they ever charged.

The battle of Christmas shopping is a time when the casualty list grows in the War on Poverty.

It's a soul-stirring experience to hear Yule carolers standing in a Los Angeles smog singing, "It Came upon a Midnight Clear."

The *way* you spend Christmas is far more important than *how much*.

One thing about Christmas shopping — it toughens you up for the January sales.

Last Christmas a stingy father told his little children that Santa Claus had been drafted into the army.

Many banks have a new kind of Christmas club in operation. The new club helps you save money to pay for last year's gifts.

Nothing destroys the Christmas spirit faster than looking for a place to park.

A family in San Francisco is reliving its Christmas holidays — the man of the house is showing colored slides of his cancelled checks.

On Christmas Eve Santa carries the bag. After Christmas dad is holding it.

"Good Will Toward Men" is the spice in the Christmas season.

Christmas is a time for exchanging a lot of things you can't afford for a lot of things you don't want.

One of the nice things about Christmas is that you can make people forget the past with a present.

There have always been some Christmas stockings that provided Santa with a few problems, but one wonders about his reaction to panty hose!

Next Christmas Santa Claus won't be the only one in the red.

If your youngster asks how Santa Claus gets into your house, tell him he comes in through a hole in daddy's wallet.

Some men refuse to believe in Santa Claus until they get married and have to be him.

By the time most fellows are in shape to play Santa Claus, the kids no longer believe in him.

When Santa Claus comes down the chimney, your money goes down the drain.

It's always charming to see little children lined up waiting to talk to the department store Santa Claus — some with parents, some with lists, and some with chicken pox.

Can you remember when Christmas was so simple that one Santa Claus could work an entire town?

Christmas is the time of the year when Santa Claus comes down the chimney and your savings go down the drain.

A man goes through three stages: he believes in Santa Claus; he doesn't believe in Santa Claus — then he is Santa Claus.

In some sections of the country Christmas shopping starts so early that Santa Claus wears Bermuda shorts.

Miscellaneous

Birthdays

Age is what makes furniture worth more and people worth less.

Which do you suppose ages faster — whiskey or the man who drinks it?

Forty is the age when you begin to realize how much fun you had when you were twenty.

By the time a man finds greener pastures, he's too old to climb the fence.

A man is usually as young as he feels but seldom as important.

The time-tested method of slowing down advancing age seems to be misrepresentation.

Age is the best possible fire extinguisher for flaming youth.

Sixty-five is the age when one acquires sufficient experience to lose his job.

To be seventy years young is sometimes more cheerful and hopeful than to be forty years old.

The least likely way for a middle-aged woman to celebrate her birthday is annually.

You can judge your age by the amount of pain you feel when you come in contact with a new idea.

The awkward age is when you are too old for the Peace Corps and too young for Social Security.

People aren't really living any longer — it just seems that way.

Regardless of their age, most folks are not as old as they hope to be.

Some people think the proper age for a man to start thinking of marriage is when he's old enough to realize he shouldn't.

Life's golden age is when the children are too old to need baby sitters and too young to borrow the family car.

By all means go ahead and mellow with age. Just be wary of getting rotten.

A California woman says her husband is at the dangerous age when all females look alike to him — desirable!

Age has nothing to do with learning new ways to be stupid.

As a man gets older he suspects that nature is plotting against him for the benefit of doctors and dentists.

Hardening of the heart ages people more quickly than hardening of the arteries.

Twenty-nine is a wonderful age for a man to be — and for a woman to stay.

The dangerous age is any time between one and ninety-nine.

It is possible that a man could live twice as long if he didn't spend the first half of his life acquiring habits that shorten the other half.

Age stiffens the joints and thickens some brains.

People usually feel they reached forty prematurely.

Many of us are at the "metallic age" — gold in our teeth, silver in our hair, and lead in our pants.

Age doesn't always bring wisdom. Sometimes age comes alone.

You're getting along in years when the only urge you feel in the spring is to climb out of your long underwear.

Life not only begins at forty — it begins to show.

Youth looks ahead, old age looks back, and middle age looks tired.

Nothing ages a man faster than trying to prove he's still as young as ever.

A man begins to show his age at about the same time he begins to show pictures of his grandchildren.

A woman likes to be reminded about her birthday — but not which one it is.

A woman usually underestimates two things — her age and how long it'll take her to get ready to go out.

Most women won't admit anything over fifty-five — whether it's age or speed.

Some of the older generation's criticism of the younger generation is heavily tinged with envy.

Some women grow old before their time trying to look young after their time.

She wasn't old, but when she lit the candles on her birthday cake, six people passed out from heat exhaustion.

It's a sign of age if you feel like the morning after the night before, and you haven't been anywhere.

The three ages of man are youth, middle age and, "My, but you are looking well."

Few women admit their age. Few men act theirs.

Our aim in life improves as we grow older, but it seems that we soon run out of ammunition.

Her birthday cake had so many candles on it she was fined for air pollution.

Cosmetics are used by teen-age girls to make them look older sooner, and by their mothers to make them look younger longer.

A gentleman in Georgia says he's at the age where he's too old for castor oil and too young for Geritol.

Gray hair usually comes along about twenty years after you thought it would make you look distinguished.

A man in Nevada says that when he was a boy his hair was light; then it turned dark, then it turned grey, then it turned loose.

In this life the old believe everything, the middle-aged suspect everything, and the young know everything.

A fellow's mistakes always bother him, especially when he realizes he's too old to repeat them.

Everybody wants to live a long time, but nobody wants to get old.

It's so sad that people are like plants — some go to seed with age and others go to pot.

Most people like the old days best — they were younger then.

Some people grow up and spread cheer; others just grow up and spread.

Our beloved country recently celebrated its two-hundredth birthday, and all we've learned in that time is how to go fast, work less, waste more, and die quicker.

The least likely way for a middle-aged woman to celebrate her birthday is annually.

George Washington was first in war, first in peace, and first to have his birthday juggled to make a long weekend.

The design on a woman's birthday cake is often very beautiful, but the arithmetic is terrible.

Birthdays are nice to have, but too many of them will kill a person.

When a man has a birthday he may take a day off. When a woman has a birthday she may take as much as five years off.

Sign in a florist's window: "Smoking, or forgetting your wife's birthday, can be hazardous to your health."

At the birthday party of a prominent spinster, many of the guests were overcome by the heat of the candles.

A woman bakes a child's birthday cake big enough to hold all the candles — and her own small enough not to.

The best way to remember your wife's birthday is to forget it once!

A diplomatic husband said to his wife, "How do you expect me to remember your birthday when you never look any older?"

If you think a woman can't keep a secret, ask one her age!

One way to get silence at a woman's bridge club is to ask who is the oldest.

The economical wife is one who uses only thirty candles on her fortieth birthday cake.

It may be true that life begins at forty, but everything else starts to wear out, fall out, or spread out.

Age is like love. It cannot be hidden.

Youth is like fashion. Both fade quickly.

There are only two things children will share willingly — communicable diseases and their mother's age.

Courage is what it takes for a woman to show friends the old Family Bible containing the date of her birth.

No one can find as many detours as a woman approaching middle age!

A diplomat remembers a lady's birthday but forgets her age.

A woman usually starts lying about her age when her face begins telling the truth about it.

About the only thing a woman is sure to remember is another woman's age.

A woman is at middle-age when she takes her high school annual out of the bookcase and hides it where the children can't find it.

The least likely way for a middle-aged woman to celebrate her birthday is annually.

Then there was the woman who was cured of her nervousness in one treatment. The doctor told her it was a sign of old age.

Most elderly women were born in the year of our Lord only knows.

There'll never be a woman president. No woman will admit to being over thirty-five.

Time waits for no man — but it stands still for a woman of thirty-five!

If medical science has done so much to add years to our lives, how come you never meet a woman who's past thirty-five?

Graduation

We rate ability in men by what they finish, not by what they attempt.

Ability without ambition is like a car without a motor.

A man seldom knows what he can do until he tries to undo what he did.

Every accomplishment, great or small, starts with the right decision, "I'll Try."

A man's accomplishment in business depends partly on whether he keeps his mind or his feet on the desk.

Don't measure yourself by what you have accomplished, but what you should have accomplished with your ability.

It's difficult to inspire others to accomplish what you haven't been willing to try.

It is simply remarkable how the apostle Paul covered so much territory and accomplished so much without a car.

A genius shoots at something no one else sees — and hits it!

To be born a gentleman is an accident — to die one is an accomplishment.

Do something. Either lead, follow, or get out of the way!

A man whose actions leave his wife speechless has really done something!

We never see the target a man aims at in life; we see only the target he hits.

Choice, not chance, determines destiny.

Some of the world's greatest deeds have been accomplished by two types of men — those who were smart enough to know it could be done, and those too dumb to know it couldn't.

Education is not received. It is *achieved.*

If it were as easy to arouse enthusiasm as it is suspicion, just think what could be accomplished!

Fear of criticism is the kiss of death in the courtship of achievement.

Having money and friends is easy. Having friends and no money is an accomplishment.

Don't forget that people will judge you by your actions, not your intentions. You may have a heart of gold — but so does a hard-boiled egg.

Begin where you are. But don't stay where you are.

You can't get anywhere unless you start.

Kind actions begin with kind thoughts.

Actions speak louder than words — and speak fewer lies.

The thing to try when all else fails is again.

Just over the hill is a beautiful valley, but you must climb the hill to see it.

Do it now! Today will be yesterday tomorrow.

Giving it another try is better than an alibi.

It's better to look where you're going than to see where you've been.

The best time to do the dishes is right after your wife tells you to.

People may doubt what you say, but they will always believe what you do.

We cannot do everything we want to do, but we should do everything God wants us to do.

Happiness is a by-product of achievement.

Money, achievement, fame, and success are important, but they are bought too dearly when acquired at the cost of health.

Hope sees the invisible, feels the intangible, and achieves the impossible.

Hope is the anchor of the soul, the stimulus to action, and the incentive to achievement.

One sure way for you to gain adherents to your cause is to start winning.

It's a mistake to try to judge a man's horsepower by the size of his exhaust.

Liberty is not a gift of God but a hard-won achievement with the help of God.

With many people telling lies is not a shortcoming but is one of their major achievements.

You cannot control the length of your life, but you can control its breadth, depth, and height.

A mistake is proof that someone was at least trying to accomplish something.

Most of us measure our success by what others haven't done.

Don't just stand there — do something!

It pays to keep your feet on the ground, but keep them moving.

Action is what you don't take when the other guy is bigger than you are.

Our actions are our own; their consequences are not.

Every action of our lives touches some chord that will vibrate in eternity.

Having a great aim in life is important. So is knowing when to pull the trigger.

If you're going to climb, you've got to grab the branches, not the blossoms.

The actions of men are the best interpreters of their thoughts.

It is a great deal better to do all the things you should do than to spend the rest of your life wishing you had.

Kind words can never die, but without kind deeds they can sound mighty sick.

Action speaks louder than words but not nearly as often.

It doesn't do any good to sit up and take notice if you keep on sitting.

The man who gets ahead is the man who does more than is necessary — and keeps on doing it.

"Push" will get a person almost everywhere — except through a door marked "pull."

Doing beats stewing.

God gives us the ingredients for our daily bread, but He expects us to do the baking.

You can do everything you ought to do.

The fellow who does things that count doesn't usually stop to count them.

There are three ways to get something done: do it yourself, hire someone to do it, or forbid your kids to do it.

No thoroughly occupied man has ever been known to be miserable.

You can never get much of anything done unless you go ahead and do it before you are ready.

Actions speak louder than words — and are just as apt to be misquoted or misinterpreted.

Some fellows dream of worthy accomplishments, while others stay awake and do them.

No one ever climbed a hill just by looking at it.

When you do something and don't want anybody to know it, it's either very good or very bad.

A man ordinarily has time to do all the things he really wants to do.

Don't sit back and take what comes. Go after what you want.

Our ship would come in much sooner if we'd only swim out to meet it.

The fellow who has an abundance of push gets along very well without pull.

If you don't climb the mountain, you can't see the view.

Where we go and what we do advertises what we are.

There's no sense aiming for a goal with no arrow in your bow.

Having the right aim in life doesn't mean a thing if you're loaded with blanks.

It is useless to have an aim in life unless one has ammunition to back it up.

Many people have a good aim in life, but for some reason they never pull the trigger.

Too many of us shoot blanks when aiming at our goals.

Think what others ought to be like, then start being like that yourself.

The surest way to gain respect is to earn it by conduct.

It's nice to be important, but it's more important to be nice.

None of us is responsible for all the things that happen to us, but we are responsible for the way we act when they do happen.

Many pious people would rather study the Bible than practice what it teaches.

It's not the load that breaks you down, it's the way you carry it.

Business is like a wheelbarrow — it stands still unless somebody pushes it.

A true test of a man's character is not what he does in the light, but what he does in the dark.

Think right, act right; it is what you think and do that makes you what you are.

A person is never what he ought to be until he is doing what he ought to be doing.

It isn't what you have, but what you are, that makes life worthwhile.

Cheerfulness is contagious, but don't wait to catch it from others. Be a carrier!

Christianity requires the participants to come down out of the grandstand and onto the playing field.

Christians are the light of the world, but the switch must be turned on.

The Christian who is pulling the oars doesn't have time to rock the boat.

The Christian's walk and talk must go together.

A genuine Christian is like a good watch: he has an open face, busy hands, is made of pure gold, is well-regulated, and is full of good works.

Some church members are like wheelbarrows — they go only when they are pushed.

A committee of three gets things done if two don't show up.

Common sense is the knack of seeing things as they are, and doing things as they ought to be done.

It might be more worthwhile if we stopped wringing our hands and started ringing our congressman.

People who live by the Golden Rule today never have to apologize for their actions tomorrow.

Few people ever get dizzy from doing too many good turns.

The smallest good deed is better than the grandest intention.

You can't reduce by talking about it. You must keep your mouth shut.

The true object of education should be to train one to think clearly and act rightly.

We make more enemies by what we say than friends by what we do.

We won't go far without enthusiasm, but neither will we go far if that's all we have.

Experience is a form of knowledge acquired in only two ways — by doing and by being done.

Failure always overtakes those who have the power to do without the will to act.

There are a lot of ways to become a failure, but never taking a chance is the most successful.

Failure is not the worst thing in the world. The very worst is not to try.

Faith without works is like an automobile without gas.

In all relationships of life, faith is worthless unless it leads to action.

Faith with works is a force. Faith without works is a farce.

The fellow who's always leaning on his family tree never seems to get out of the woods.

No farmer ever plowed a field by turning it over in his mind.

Even if a farmer intends to loaf, he gets up in time to get an early start.

The one thing worse than a quitter is the man who is afraid to start.

The only thing we have to fear is not doing something about the fear we have.

Promises may get friends, but it is performance that keeps them.

We make our future by the best use of the present.

Genius is 1 percent inspiration and 99 percent perspiration.

Knowing without doing is like plowing without sowing.

The best time to do something worthwhile is between yesterday and tomorrow.

A man's conscience tells him what he shouldn't do — but it does not keep him from doing it.

Those who can — do. Those who can't — criticize.

You don't have time to criticize when you harmonize, sympathize, and evangelize.

If it were not for the doers, the critics would soon be out of business.

Your creed may be interesting but your deeds are much more convincing.

The Golden Rule is of little value unless you realize that you must make the first move.

Looking for trouble is wasted energy. All a guy has to do is to sit down and wait.

Going to heaven is like riding a bicycle — you must either go on or get off.

The hope is that some day the Christian ideal will be put into practice.

Unexpressed ideas are of no more value than kernels in a nut before it has been cracked.

Some people entertain ideas; others put them to work.

A "sensational new idea" is sometimes just an old idea with its sleeves rolled up.

Good ideas need landing gear as well as wings.

Ideas are funny things. They don't work unless you do.

Every time one man expresses an idea, he finds ten men who thought of it before — but they only thought.

An idea is more than information; it is information with legs, and — it is headed somewhere.

You can't make a hit with the bat on your shoulder.

There is nothing more terrifying than ignorance in action.

Good intentions die unless they are executed.

Never judge a man's actions until you know his motives.

A little knowledge that acts is worth infinitely more than much knowledge that is idle.

Leisure is a beautiful garment, but it will not do for constant wear.

It isn't how high you go in life that counts, but *how* you got there.

When all the affairs of life are said and done, there is more said than done.

Works, not words, are the proof of love.

Some people never make a mistake, nor do they ever make anything else.

A mistake proves somebody stopped talking long enough to do something.

Even when opportunity knocks, a man still has to get off his seat and open the door.

Never waste time reflecting on opportunities you have missed. While thus reflecting you might miss some more.

Man's maximum achievement often falls short of God's minimum demands.

The world has finally achieved perpetual commotion.

After saying our prayers we ought to do something to make them come true.

The right angle to approach a difficult problem is the "try-angle."

Commencement is when the college students who learned all the answers discover that there are a new set of questions.

Commencement speaker in Michigan: "My advice to young people who are going out in the world today — don't go!"

All progress is due to those who were not satisfied to let well enough alone.

People are won to your religious beliefs less by description than by demonstration.

For success, try aspiration, inspiration, and perspiration.

If you itch for success, keep on scratching.

The man who fails while trying to do good has more honor than he who succeeds by accident.

Before proceeding with a difficult task, stop and think. Then remember to start again.

It's about time for folks to carry this do-it-yourself craze to thinking.

Acting without thinking is a lot like shooting without aiming.

A spoken word and a thrown stone cannot be recalled.

Our words may hide our thoughts, but our actions will reveal them.

Words should be used as tools of communication and not as a substitute for action.

You can't clean up this old world with soft soap; it takes grit.

The world we live in is old-fashioned. It still judges a man by what he does.

It is not only what you do, but also what you don't do, for which you are accountable.

The only thing in life achieved without effort is failure.

You must first be a believer if you would be an achiever.

The only thing some people can achieve on their own is dandruff.

Today's preparation determines tomorrow's achievement.

Some men achieve distinction by the kind of car they drive — others by the kind of wife that is driving them.

If you want a place in the sun, you will have to expect some blisters.

It is when we forget ourselves that we do things that are most likely to be remembered.

No man is fully accomplished until he has acquired the ability to attend to his own business.

There are four steps to accomplishment: Plan purposefully. Prepare prayerfully. Proceed positively. Pursue persistently.

You can't make a place for yourself under the sun if you keep sitting in the shade of the family tree.

There are still a few people who believe in gittin' up and gittin', while a great many prefer sittin' down and sittin'.

Vacations

The best place to spend your vacation is just inside your income.

Vacations are easy to plan — the boss tells you when, and the wife tells you where.

If you can't get away for a vacation, you can get the same feeling by staying home and tipping every third person you see.

Frankly, no one needs a vacation as much as the person who just had one.

Spend your vacation next year in your own backyard and your friends will know what you are — sensible, home-loving, and broke.

Your vacation is over when your money is spent, and so are you.

The one book that really tells you where you can go on your vacation is your pocketbook.

When a worried, haggard patient enters the doctor's office, the doctor hardly knows whether to prescribe a vacation or treat the patient for the one he has just had.

The ideal summer resort is where the fish bite and the mosquitoes don't.

A vacation is a success if we manage to change the color of the circles under our eyes from black to tan.

Vacation is a brief period of recreation, preceded by a period of anticipation, and followed by a period of recuperation.

A vacation is something you need by the time you finish paying for one.

One reason many of us can't afford a European vacation is because our dollars made the trip without us.

You're getting old when you're on vacation and your energy runs out before your money does.

The question we all must face sooner or later is how to fit a long vacation into a short bankroll.

Nothing makes time pass faster than vacations and short-term loans.

Why is it that a tourist will travel thousands of miles to get away from people — just so he can send cards saying, "Wish you were here"?

A vacation is what you take if you can't take what you've been taking.

The world is full of cheap vacation spots. The trouble is that it costs a lot of money to get there.

People usually go on a vacation to forget — and when they open their luggage they learn what is was they forgot.

The trouble with most vacation spots is they don't have the same girls you saw in their ads.

Vacation means two weeks on the sand and the rest of the year on the rocks.

Advice to vacationers: Don't overtax yourself. The government will do it for you.

Those who say you can't take it with you have never seen a family car packed for a vacation.

Vacation time is when the highway department closes all the roads and opens up all the detours.

Wouldn't it be nice if two weeks on vacation seemed to last as long as two weeks on a diet?

For a vacation some will go to the mountains, while others go to the seashore, but most of us will go in the hole.

Some people take everything on a vacation except their manners.

Vacation is a time when you get away from the people and places you love best, so you can put up with them when you get back.

A Mississippi couple couldn't decide whether to use their vacation money for a trip abroad or a steak at home.

Some people who went on a vacation last summer made the usual mistake — they took along more clothing than they used and less money than they needed.

A vacation is usually nothing but a sunburn at premium prices.

You don't have to vacation at the seashore to get soaked.

A vacation is two weeks of fun followed by weeks of short funds.

A business executive in Denver gave his employees long vacations to find out which ones he could do without.

A girl certainly has a wide choice of vacations. She can go to the mountains and see the scenery, or go to the beach and be the scenery.

Even if your vacation isn't long, you'll come back short.

The biggest obstacles to planning this year's vacation are the payments still due on last year's.

Change is what a person wants on a vacation — and a lot of currency too.

If you have not taken a vacation by now, you can at least figure what you've saved by listening to friends who have just returned.

One of the most common disruptions of marital bliss is the choice of where to spend a vacation. What this country needs is an ocean in the mountains.

A vacation makes you feel good enough to return to work — and so poor you have to.

The fellow who first said, "Spend your vacation..." never realized how right he was.

Why not spend your vacation in Las Vegas? You can't beat the sunshine, the climate, or the slot machines.

Next summer one-third of the nation will be ill-housed and ill-fed — but they'll call it a vacation.

The only thing that goes faster than vacation time is vacation cash.

Some people's idea of roughing it is to spend their vacation in a small town where they can get only one channel on TV.

The ideal summer resort is where the fish bite and the mosquitoes don't.

Vacation is a system whereby people who are merely tired become exhausted.

At today's prices people don't take vacations — vacations take people.

85

Thousands of people will not be going on vacation this year. In fact, many of us can't even afford to stay at home.

You can enjoy a glorious vacation and stay within your budget — but not both in the same summer.

A Kansas couple couldn't afford a winter vacation last year. However, they did save enough money to turn up their thermostat for one weekend.

There's nothing so dull as going on the kind of vacation we can afford.

Let's hope we can take our vacation before postcards go up again.

Vacations are a little like love — anticipated with relish, experienced with inconvenience, and remembered with nostalgia.

Note to summer vacationers: When you're advised to travel light, they mean luggage, not your wallet.

Most people could live within their incomes if they were as economical all year round as they are right after their vacations.

If you want a successful vacation, take half the clothes you figured on and twice the money.

Any guy who looks completely exhausted should take a vacation — or has!

The trouble with vacations is that it takes such a long time paying for such a short time playing.

Some of the best vacations this past summer were spent at home, where you don't have to tip for lousy service, and the insolence is free.

A vacation is a holiday from everything except expenses.

It's pretty hard to take a vacation from doing nothing.

A Texan, just back home from a Nevada vacation, says he underwent a bit of "Las Vegas Surgery." He had his bankroll painlessly removed.

Don't tell the tired-looking person he needs a vacation — the chances are he just had one.

A vacation is a two week's experience where money and time race each other until both are exhausted.

Summer vacations get kids tan, mothers in the pink, and fathers in the red.

A vacation consists of equal parts of sunburn, sore muscles, and discomfort.

Weddings

A young Georgia husband is mad at the minister who performed his marriage ceremony. The minister asked his bride, "Do you take this man for better, or probably worse?"

To the bachelor, horror films are pictures of a wedding.

The best and surest way to save a marriage from divorce is not to show up for the wedding.

There's nothing like a little exercise to change a man's life — especially if it's a walk down a church aisle.

A wedding cake is the only cake that can give you indigestion for the rest of your life.

Give a girl enough rope and she'll ring the wedding bell.

Most girls seem to marry men like their fathers. Maybe that's the reason so many mothers cry at weddings.

Then there was the good little girl who had been saying no so long that she almost loused up her wedding ceremony.

A wedding is a ceremony at which a man loses complete control of himself.

Psychiatrists tell us that girls tend to marry men who are like their fathers. Now we know why mothers cry at weddings.

It takes only a few words mumbled in church and you're married. It takes only a few words mumbled in your sleep and you're divorced.

A recent wedding between two hypochondriacs was very touching. They exchanged vows and symptoms.

The most difficult years of marriage are those following the wedding.

In spite of all the plans for world peace, there will probably be the usual number of June weddings.

Preacher at wedding: "If this check for one dollar clears, I now pronounce you husband and wife."

A candidate's promises aren't really extravagant when you compare them to a bridegroom's.

The entire civil war was covered with fewer photographs than are taken at the average wedding today.

Nothing seems to make a wedding so expensive as being the father of the bride.

Not all weddings planned for June will end in divorce. Some won't even get past making out the guest list.

At an Alabama wedding the bride was so homely everybody kissed the groom.

Some people never go to a wedding. They can't stand to see a man deprived of his human rights.

A father in Georgia called his local IRS office to ask if he could deduct the cost of his daughter's wedding as a "total loss"?

In Hollywood the bride tossing the bouquet is just as likely to be the next one to get married as the girl who catches it.

A tenth wedding anniversary is difficult to celebrate. It's too soon to brag and too late to complain.

It's unlucky to postpone a wedding, but not if you keep on doing it.

A Hollywood wedding is one where they take each other for better or worse — but not for long.

Weddings have become so costly that it's now the father of the bride who breaks down and weeps.

The man leads the woman to the altar at a wedding ceremony — after which his leadership ends.

The wedding is a ceremony where the bridegroom starts kissing the bride and the other fellows stop.

Have you heard about those computer arranged weddings? The couple promises not to fold, spindle, or mutilate?

A young woman in Missouri reports she had an economical wedding last year. The invitations were not engraved — they were xeroxed.

Most accidents occur in the home. Many men use this as an excuse to stay out late.

A Hollywood actress is now teaching a course on educational TV — husbandry!

There's an unusual actress in Hollywood — she's signed more marriage certificates than autographs.

On TV talk shows the Hollywood actresses always seem to mention either their last picture or their next husband.

Many actresses won't wear a dress that's not original, but they'll take a secondhand husband.

A Chicago actress says she's been so busy planning her sixth marriage she hasn't time to cook for her fifth husband.

Advertising is a good deal like marriage. There may be a better way, but what is it?

Any man who has to ask for advice probably isn't married.

Advice to the bridegroom: No matter how she treats you, always try to look a little hurt.

Some people think the proper age for a man to start thinking of marriage is when he's old enough to realize he shouldn't.

Many a husband has learned that an ironclad alibi isn't as effective as a diamond-studded one.

When you see a married couple who's coming down the street, the one two or three steps ahead is the one who's mad.

Married couples who claim they've never had an argument in forty years either have poor memories or a very dull life to recall.

When you're arguing with your wife, make absolutely sure you're right — and then let the matter drop.

Romance goes out the window when she stops knitting and starts needling.

There's nothing like a marriage to break up a beautiful romance.

The kind of music people should have in their homes is domestic harmony.

A real optimist is the husband who goes to the marriage bureau to see if his license has expired.

Two Texas political candidates were having a heated debate. One shouted, "What about the powerful interests that control you?" The other screamed back, "You leave my wife out of this."

Romance often begins by a splashing waterfall and ends over a leaky sink.

Romance is like a game of chess — one false move and you're mated.

Scientists tell us that the most devastating thing in the world is the A-bomb; the second most devastating thing is coming home with lipstick on your collar.

Another thing marriage brings out in a lot of men is silence.

A marriage counselor says a man should make his wife a silent partner in all his business affairs. It would be a great trick if he could do it.

Notice on a new TV set: "Warning — extended watching of basketball and baseball games may be harmful to your marriage."

What a married couple should save for their old age is each other.

Time separates the best of friends, and so does money — and don't forget marriage!

The most impressive evidence of tolerance is a golden wedding anniversary.

If a woman can be a sweetheart, valet, audience, cook, and nurse, she is qualified for marriage.

A husband and wife in Montana make it a point not to argue over anything not worth arguing about. Of course, this leads to some dandy fights over whether or not a subject is worthwhile.

The argument you just won with your wife isn't over yet.

The trouble with marriage is not the institution. It's the personnel.

Time changes things. Nowadays the couple has the honeymoon first, and if it's a success, they have the engagement, and if that works out all right, they *may* have a wedding.

Description of a newlywed couple: His aim is to save money. Her ambition is to spoil his aim.

You can always recognize the newlywed in the supermarket. She's the one who squeezes the can of soup to see if it's fresh.

Most modern-day brides have the makings of a good wife, but they haven't been "kitchen-tested."

It's hard for some of these new wives to get used to being whistled for instead of at.

A woman marries the first time for love, the second time for companionship, the third time for support, and the rest of the time from habit.

A woman in Ohio says she's wearing her wedding ring on the wrong finger because she married the wrong man.

People cry at weddings because they have been through it and know it's no laughing matter.

After paying for the wedding, about the only thing a father has left to give away is the bride.

The only state that permits a woman to work more than eight hours a day is the state of matrimony.

There is nothing so unromantic as a seasick bride.

Arguing with your wife is as useless as trying to blow out a lightbulb.

After winning an argument with his wife, the wisest thing a man can do is apologize.

The hottest arguments over Canasta start after the guests depart.

There are a lot more marital arguments over a wink than a mink.

A divorce is what happens when what you thought was a marriage turns out to be a conglomerate.

The divorce rate would be lower if, instead of marrying for better or worse, people would marry for good.

You have only to mumble a few words in church to get married and a few in your sleep to get divorced.

Love is the quest, marriage the conquest, divorce the inquest.

Many divorces are caused by the marriage of two people who are in love with themselves.

A wealthy father didn't know what to give his daughter as a wedding present, so he promised to pay for her divorce.

Some men believe in dreams until they marry one.

Sometimes an adult education begins with a teen-age marriage.

We've had adult education for several thousand years. It's called marriage.

An executive refused an employee's request for a raise, adding, "I know you can't get married on what I pay you — and someday you'll thank me."

It's impossible for a man to make a fool of himself without knowing it — not if he's married.

Faith is better company than imagination for the wife whose husband fails to come home on time.

An Arizona wit says people shouldn't get married on Sunday because it's not right to gamble on a Holy Day.

Marriage often results when a man meets a woman who understands him. So does divorce.

Making marriage work is like operating a farm. You have to start all over again each morning.

Bachelors have no idea what married bliss is, and that's also true of a lot of husbands.

Las Vegas has all kinds of gambling devices, such as dice, roulette, slot machines — and wedding chapels.

It may be that bachelors make more mistakes than married men — but they don't make the big one.

A bachelor is a rolling stone that gathers no boss.

A bachelor may have no buttons on his shirt, but a married man often has no shirt.

Many a bachelor longs for a wife who will take care of him — and so does many a husband.

Some banks guarantee maximum interest rates for several years, which is more than a marriage license can do.

Bigamy is having one wife too many — monogamy is often the same.

Judging from some of the specimens they select, can you blame brides for blushing?

The husband who boasts that he never made a mistake has a wife who did.

A Hollywood star boasts he's been happily married for twenty years. Of course, it took him five marriages to do it.

Brains are what a man looks for in a wife, after not using any in selecting one.

A married couple usually works out a budget together and then breaks it separately.

Not too long ago business got so bad that some men went bankrupt, and some went back to their wives.

A baby may not be able to lift very much, but it can hold a marriage together.

Children always know when company is in the living room — they can hear their mother laughing at their father's jokes.

It's amazing how many things a girl can do without until she gets married.

One way a girl can stop a man from making love to her is to marry him.

Marriage is seldom successful unless both parties get better mates than they deserve.

The honeymoon is over when the bride begins to suspect that she was never anything to him but a tax deduction.

After the honeymoon the girl usually stops wondering what she should wear and starts wondering how long it will last.

The honeymoon is over when he finds out he married a big spender and she finds out she didn't.

A honeymoon is the short period between the bridal toast and the burnt toast.

The honeymoon is over when you realize that everything she says or cooks disagrees with you.

The honeymoon is a period of doting between dating and debating.

It's easy to spot honeymooners in Las Vegas. The man kisses his wife even when he's losing.

The honeymoon is over when a wife stops making a fuss *over* her husband and begins to make a fuss *with* him.

The honeymoon is definitely over when all the babytalk around the house is done only by the baby.

A woman in Arizona married so late in life that Medicare paid for her honeymoon.

Gentlemen prefer blondes -- especially gentlemen who are married to brunettes.

You'll never convince a newlywed bride that someday she might prefer a dishwasher to a mink coat.

When a girl marries she gives up the attention of several men for the inattention of one.

When it comes to broken marriages most husbands will split the blame — half his wife's fault, and half her mother's.

If you're wondering what happened to the old-fashioned girl, you'll probably find her at home with her husband and children.

The old-fashioned mother who saved her wedding togs for her daughter now has a daughter who tries to make them outlast three husbands.

Common sense could prevent a great many divorces; but, on the other hand, it could also prevent a great many marriages.

The woman who complains about the man she married should realize that she could have caught a bigger fish if she had used better bait.

A Missouri man complains that he was married fifteen years ago by a Justice of the Peace, and since that time he has had neither justice nor peace.

A dish towel will certainly wipe a contented look off a married man's face.

At a convention the "delegate-at-large" is the man who has come without his wife.

Why are husbands and wives more courteous to strangers than to each other?

More and more lovely courtships sail into the sea of matrimony, and finally sink into the rocky storms of divorce.

Courtship, unlike proper punctuation, is a period before a sentence.

Before criticizing your wife's faults, you must remember it may have been those very defects which prevented her from getting a better husband than the one she married.

When a man decides to marry, it may be the last decision he'll ever be allowed to make.

When a girl casts her bread upon the waters, she expects it to come back to her in the shape of a wedding cake.

It's true that some people get divorced for trivial reasons. But, then, some of them got married for trivial reasons.

Too many people are finding it easier to get married than to stay married.

There is entirely too much worrying about unhappy marriages. All marriages are happy. It's only living together afterward that causes the trouble.

You can send your marriage to an early grave with a series of little digs.

Marriage is the difference between painting the town and painting the back porch.

Sign in a marriage bureau window: "Out to lunch — think it over!"

Engaged couples should realize that marriage will never be as good as *she* believes or as bad as *he* suspects.

Marriage is the world's most expensive way of discovering your faults.

Many people who suddenly realize that they can't afford to get married already are.

A couple recently had their marriage annulled, and sued the officiating minister for malpractice.

Before marriage the three little words are, "I love you." After marriage they are, "Let's eat out."

Marriage is a nice sort of life for a husband to lead — if only his wife would let him do a little leading.

A beefstew marriage is when she's always beefing, and he's always stewed.

Getting married is like buying on credit. You see something, you like it, you make it your own, and you pay for it later.

Marriage is a case of two people agreeing to change each other's habits.

A man in Montana has been married so many times his last marriage license was made out TO WHOM IT MAY CONCERN.

Marriage is an alliance between two people — one who never remembers a birthday and the other who never forgets them.

It's easy for a married couple to acquire mutual interests. All *he* has to do is what *she* likes.

A marriage seldom goes on the rocks when a couple finds something in common to laugh about. For instance, there's the old wedding pictures!

One nice thing about being a man is that you don't have to kiss somebody who hasn't shaved in three days.

A well-informed man is one whose wife has just told him what she thinks of him.

There would be a lot more happy marriages if husbands tried to understand their wives and wives tried to understand football.

Marriage is like arthritis. You have to learn to live with it.

What frightens most men about marriage is not another mouth to feed — but another one to listen to!

Most men think they're marrying a cook; most women think they're marrying a banker.

Some men who say they're not interested in marriage have wives sitting home alone to prove it.

Marriage is perhaps the most expensive way to get advice for nothing.

In most marriages the husband is the provider and the wife is the decider.

The person who marries for money usually earns every penny of it.

When you see how willingly some young men go to the marriage bureau, the idea of a volunteer army doesn't seem so far-fetched.

Marriage is like horseradish — men praise it with tears in their eyes.

When a man and woman marry they become one — and they spend the rest of their lives trying to find out which one.

The thought of marriage frightens a lot of bachelors — and a few husbands too!

More marriages will be inevitable if postage continues to increase. It'll be cheaper to marry the girl than to write to her.

Marriage may be inspired by music, soft words, and perfume; but its security is manifest in work, consideration, respect, and well-fried bacon.

Some of our modern girls turn a man's head with charm — and his stomach with their cooking.

The girl who remembers her first kiss now has a daughter who can't even remember her first husband.

Girls who fall in love with a fellow at first sight sometimes wish they had taken a second look.

Some girls get married for financial security; others get divorced for the same reason.

More golden wedding anniversaries would be celebrated if more couples practiced the Golden Rule.

Genuine happiness is when a wife sees a double chin on her husband's old girl friend.

Hollywood is just one great big family. Everybody is related by marriage — or soon will be.

In Hollywood a happy marriage is one in which the husband loves his wife more than somebody else's.

Some Hollywood people compare marriage to eating salted peanuts — it's hard to stop at one.

In Hollywood they figure a marriage has a chance of succeeding if the couple leaves the church together.

Girls expect money with marriage because they have difficulty finding anything else worthwhile in a man.

Marriage was formerly a contract, but it's now regarded as a ninety-day option.

Nothing makes a marriage rust like distrust.

A typical marriage is where the husband keeps his mouth shut and his checkbook open.

There's one point at which both husband and wife are in perfect agreement — he thinks nothing is too good for her, and so does she.

Marriage is too often a case where cupidity meets stupidity.

The average man has probably thought twice about running away from home — once as a child and once as a husband.

A happy home is one in which each spouse entertains the possibility that the other may be right, though neither believes it.

A mother may hope that her daughter will get a better husband than she did, but she knows her son will never get as good a wife as his father did.

On his fiftieth wedding anniversary an Arkansas husband explained his happy marriage, "At home I rule the roost — and my wife rules the rooster."

God gave women a sense of humor — so they could understand the jokes they married.

Husbands are like wood fires. When unattended they go out.

The ideal of some men is to marry a rich girl who is too proud to have her husband work.

Many a girl who elopes wishes later she had just let her imagination run away with her.

A kiss is what a husband struggled for before marriage and what his wife struggles for after marriage.

Almost everybody gets married while they're in Las Vegas. They figure as long as they're on a losing streak they might as well go all the way.

It is better to be laughed at for not being married than to be unable to laugh because you are.

If a man is too lazy to think for himself, he should get married!

The way the cost of living and taxes are today, you might as well marry for love.

Love is the beautiful story, and marriage is the "talkie" version of it.

Love intoxicates a man; marriage often sobers him.

The bonds of matrimony are worthless unless the interest is kept up.

Even the thought of embarking on the sea of matrimony makes some men seasick.

The sea of matrimony is where many a poor fish gets hooked with his own line.

Speaking of "doubtful states" — there's the state of matrimony!

Some people don't take much stock in the bonds of matrimony.

On the rough sea of matrimony, many a husband or wife has vanished overboard.

Some of those who embark on the sea of matrimony know little about navigation.

The sea of matrimony is so called because husbands have such a hard time keeping their heads above water.

Some folks get into the sea of matrimony on a wave of enthusiasm.

The bonds of matrimony are like any other bond — they take a while to mature.

The state of matrimony is one state that permits a woman to work eighteen hours a day.

The medical world has its problems. It's hard to give a man shock treatments once he's seen his wife in hair curlers.

Even the men who aren't meek get married and get that way.

Memory is what tells a man his wedding anniversary was yesterday.

A woman always remembers where and when she got married; a man sometimes forgets why!

There was a middle-aged man in Ohio who married an eighteen-year-old girl. He didn't know whether to take her on a honeymoon or send her to camp.

Money is something a man saves so he can get married — and then be broke the rest of his life.

On the matrimonial sea, the hand that rocks the cradle seldom rocks the boat.

A model marriage is one in which the wife is the treasure and the husband the treasury.

One reason why so many marriages are failures is that so many inexperienced people get into them.

It's difficult to tell who gets the most pleasure out of marriage, the preacher who ties the knot, or the lawyer who severs it.

Why shouldn't a woman take her husband's name? She takes everything else!

A serious impediment to a successful marriage these days is the difficulty of supporting both the government and a wife on one small income.

Women wear rings to show they're married, while men wear last year's clothes for the same reason.

A married man was once accused of being a deserter, but it turned out that he was only a refugee.

Success in marriage is more than finding the right person. It's also a matter of being the right person.

Marriage is like canned hash — you've got to take a chance.

If a man's wife is his "better half," and he marries twice, what happens to him mathematically?

The story of some marriages should be told in a scrapbook.

Many marriages crack up when the bill collector cracks down.

The unhappiness in some marriages is due to illness — they're sick of each other!

Getting married is one mistake every man should make.

Many married couples never go out. The husband sits in front of the TV set and smokes. The wife sits in front of the TV set and fumes.

Marriage is like twirling a baton, turning handsprings, or eating with chopsticks. It looks easy till you try it.

A man in Oklahoma admitted he lied on his income-tax return — he listed himself as the head of the household!

There's many a girl who got married because she didn't like to spend her evenings alone — and then got a divorce for the same reason.

Trial marriages may be dangerous. They could lead to the real thing.

Another reason for unhappy marriages is that men can't fool their wives like they could their mothers.

It takes at least two people to make a marriage — a single girl and an anxious mother.

Something every couple should save for their old age is marriage.

Marriages are made in heaven — so are thunder and lightning.

Anybody who thinks marriage is a fifty-fifty proposition doesn't understand women or fractions.

Some wives believe the secret of a happy marriage is doing things together — like opening a joint checking account.

An Ohio woman reports that she has a "glow-worm" marriage. The glow has gone, but the worm remains.

All forms of gambling are frowned upon by preachers — except marriage.

If all gambling were illegal, we would all have to stop driving cars and getting married.

Marriage entitles a woman to the protection of a stalwart man who'll hold the ladder while she paints the ceiling.

A producer in Hollywood plans a film entitled "Marriage, Hollywood Style." It will be short.

When a boy marries, his mother thinks he's throwing himself away, and his sisters think the girl is.

A sure sign your marriage is slipping is when you start bidding against each other at auctions.

An Oklahoma woman refused to marry her boyfriend for religious reasons. He was broke, and she worshipped money.

Marriage is too often a process whereby love ripens into vengeance.

Some men get married because they're tired of going to the laundromat, eating in restaurants, and wearing socks with holes in them. Other men get divorces for the same reasons.

Marriages are made in heaven, but they are lived on earth.

A good many things are easier said than done — including the marriage ritual.

What marriage needs is more open minds and fewer open mouths.

A marriage may be a holy wedlock or an unholy deadlock.

To marry a woman for her beauty is like buying a house for its paint.

An engagement is an urge on the verge of a merge.

Fewer marriages would skid if more who said "I do" did.

If men acted after marriage as they do during courtship there would be fewer divorces — and more bankruptcies.

The best things to get out of marriage are children.

One does not find happiness in marriage, but takes happiness into marriage.

The "good old days" date back to the time when marriage produced more triangles on the clothesline than in the courtroom.

Marriage brings music into a man's life — he learns to play second fiddle.